A BEACON OF LIGHT ON GRIEF

Cracking the Code
Using This "How To" Handbook Guide

TEMPLATES GUIDES FOR

INDIVIDUALS
Gather Family Information/Plan for Funeral Service

CHURCHES
First Call Templates/Creating a Bereavement Ministry

DOCTORS
Patients/Hospice, Bequeaths/Caregivers/Health

FUNERAL HOMES
Church Protocol for Ministers/Funeral Director/Family

LAWYERS
Estate Planning and Wills

THELMA MANNING HALL, Ph.D.

A Beacon of Light on Grief

© 2019 by Thelma Manning Hall, Ph.D.

All rights reserved.

No portion of this book may be reproduced, stored in a retrieval system, or transmitted in any form or by means of electronic, mechanical, photocopy, recording, scanning, or another excerpt for brief quotations in critical reviews or articles, without the prior written permission of the publisher.

ISBN: 978-1-948638-57-9 (paperback)

Library of Congress Copyright Registration Number:
TX 8-773-037

Published by

Fideli Publishing, Inc.
119 W. Morgan St.
Martinsville, IN 46151
www.FideliPublishing.com

Acknowledgments

My heart of gratefulness and thankfulness to each of you:

Pastor Clinton House for your encouragement and support to serve as the Bereavement Ministry Director, Coordinator and a leader at the Mountaintop Faith Ministries, Las Vegas, Nevada

To Bereavement Ministry Team, thanks for all your support with me over the many years of serving our congregation together.

To John McCall, Leak Funeral Home, Chicago, Illinois, for allowing me to ask your guidance and pull from your stability in the industry for many years.

To Donald Weaver, Professional Services, St. Louis, Missouri, for encouraging me to write the book, for your guidance and influence and for answering my questions.

To Beverly Burton, Palms Mortuary, Las Vegas, Nevada for your dedicated hours of editing and many meaningful discussions.

To Joan Norris, for all your time, talent and knowledge in the technology field.

To Steve Wesley, many thanks to you for your encouragement and for sharing your vast knowledge of intellectual technology with me to make this book possible.

To my husband, thank you for monitoring my hours of input and for insisting on proper rest while driven by a labor of love to put this book together for people who need this information all over the world.

Special thanks to Robin Surface, my publisher, for being my bedrock, for her diligence and making this book possible.

Table of Contents

Chapter I: Individuals and Personal Guidance

    A. Secure Vital Statistics

    B. Paying Bills

    C. Collection of Documents and Paperwork

    D. Decide and Arrange within Few Hours

    E. Plan to Notify as Soon as Possible

Chapter II: Family Information

    A Guide to the Information You Need to Gather, including:

Chapter III: Membership Information Mortuary & Funeral Information

Chapter XIII: Online Profile Sheets and Templates

The Watch Tower
(an allegory)

As tall as the watch tower stands
So is your statue.

As far as the beacon's light shines
So does your brightness.

The watch tower stands tall to guide water craft
Safely ashore.

The beacon's light gives hope of safely reaching
Its destination.

You stand tall in statue to see afar
Your light shines bright with
Purpose, hope, love
And will guide all of us
Through the contrary winds in life.

The master of land, ocean and sea,
Calms the waters and the winds.

There is hope.

Stand tall
Be a bright light!

How to Use This Book

Chapter One, Individual Information helps you to get started documenting, in writing, how you and your financial affairs are to be handled; and how you want to be treated, if in hospital or hospice; and your decision for final disposition.

Create your personal legacy guide to give your family a detailed list of all your personal information, social security number, bank, property and anything you own. Family needs to:

a. Know vital statistics

b. Know to pay for services

c. Know location of documents and paperwork

d. Know information for arrangements

Chapter Two, How to Make your Preparations for a Funeral Service prior to the loss of a loved one. When all the pertinent information is gathered and the location is known before it is needed, there is no uncertainty for the family when trying to secure certain necessary data.

The family should know:

a. The funeral home selected;

b. Coordinate with church and funeral home, and

c. Know specific funeral notifications.

From the data collected in Chapters One and Two, the family can move forward to implement your loved one's decisions.

In Chapter Three, Mortuary or Funeral Homes will process information based on information in Chapter One, and Chapter Two.

The family must sign a release form so the funeral home can obtain the release of the remains of your loved one; a consignment form is sometimes needed for an insurance company to use policies to pay the funeral home. The number of death certificates ordered is based on how many companies or agencies will require an original death certificate: a. insurance policies, b. pensions, c. social security and d. veteran facilities. The template includes information which can be used to create a death certificate that is coordinated with the doctor, the health department, and the cemetery.

Chapter Four, Church Protocol; Chapter Five, Funeral Programs; and Chapter Six, Church Traditional Funeral Protocol, will interact and work together.

Chapter Four, Church Protocol, is your first contact with the church. The template consist of seven parts to help with necessary information for putting together the church funeral service.

Chapter Five, Funeral Programs, has a template that will help with putting a Memorial or a Traditional Program together and has suggested poems to use. A specific template for writing an obituary will help guide you through what is often most challenging when information is not readily available.

Chapter Six, Church Traditional Funeral Protocol, helps the minister, funeral director and the family to precede to a holding area at the church and the proper line up for entering and departing the sanctuary.

Chapter Seven, Hosting Funeral Services for other churches happens when a family wants to have a service and the church maybe too small. This requires the families to reach out to another church to host the service.

Chapter Eight, Church Bereavement Checklist and the Church Standard Operating Procedures and Chapter Four works well together and serves to inform each ministry of their duties for a funeral service.

Chapter Nine, The Church Bereavement Ministry Coordinator has a specific role in the church to give guidance, show compassion, console and comfort the family.

If a church does not have a bereavement ministry, there is a template, to use as a guide, to help create the ministry; provides qualifications for a leader; Do and Don't for consoling the bereaved family; provides a dress code.

Chapter One, Individual Information; Chapter Two How to Plan Prior to a Funeral Service; Chapter Three, Mortuary and Funeral Homes; and Chapter Ten, Doctors, working together will help implement your loved one's wishes without a lot of confusion.

Chapter Ten, Doctors, consists of a checklist for caregivers and how to protect yourself. There is a template for an Advance Medical Directive or Medical Power of Attorney plus a Living Will. Secure pamphlet from the doctor for Five Wishes

Chapter Two, Gather Financial Information; Chapter Three, Financial Data and Personal Statistics; and Chapter Eleven includes enlightening information on finances.

Chapter Eleven, Lawyers can provide information on Power of Attorney, Estate Planning, Financial Information, Wills & Trusts and Revocable & Irrevocable Trusts and Estate Planning Value Calculations. Provided is a template, to be used as a guide, for Estate Planning and Financial information.

Chapter Twelve, Insurance, consist of basic information on insurance types for life, whole, term, pre-paid burial and annuities. Provided are two templates to list Life Insurance Policies, and Property Insurance Policies.

Chapter Thirteen, Social Media Profiles Information. Templates are provided to record name of company, user id and passwords.

Our Hope and Expectation

Loss of a loved one from our family is a time when sorrow grips our hearts. Not understanding the sudden loss of a loved one is why families seek consolation. The questions, "Why my Family?" and "Why did my loved one have to die?" are often asked. Our hope is in Christ Jesus and our expectation is to see our loved ones again, therefore the answer to these questions is explained in the Word of God, I Thessalonians 4:13 through 18 (KJV):

> [13]But I would not have you to be ignorant, brethren, concerning them which are asleep, that ye sorrow not, even as others which have no hope.
>
> [14]For if we believe that Jesus died and rose again, even so them also which sleep in Jesus will God bring with him.
>
> [15]For this we say unto you by the word of the Lord, that we which are alive and remain unto the coming of the Lord shall not prevent them which are asleep.
>
> [16]For the lord himself shall descend from heaven with a shout, with the voice of an archangel, and with the trump of God: and the dead in Christ shall rise first:
>
> [17]Then we which are alive and remain shall be caught up together with them in the clouds, to meet the Lord in the air: and so shall we ever be with the Lord.
>
> [18]Wherefore comfort one another with these words.

Preface

This "How To" Handbook will empower you with the help of templates to help guide you through the many facets of the funeral processes and will help you in preparing for a funeral service. It will provide insight to help you plan, in advance, for the unknown.

We have lost a loved one and we select the proper dress for our loved one, surround the body with flowers, using soft lights and using words like he passed away or departed this life instead of he died, but, try as we might, we cannot make death something beautiful.

It is true, having a funeral service, does not lessen the pain, and the tears flow as the funeral service provides us with closure and helps us acknowledge that death is final.

When one does not have sufficient funds for a traditional funeral service, one can make the decision to cremate their loved one. However, our grieving process is just as painful if not more because of inadequate planning.

There are ways to set up a fundraising account called a "GoFundMe" account and can be accessed on internet at https://pages.gofundme.com/online-fundraising. You may ask what is GoFundMe? Answer, GoFundMe is the world's largest online fundraising platform with more than $5 Billion raised so far.

How does it work:

1. Create your story and attract support.

2. Share with friends and family on Facebook, Twitter, and email sharing made easy.

3. Easily accept donations. Receive your money by requesting a check or bank transfer.

After you read this book from cover to cover, you will be challenged to get started on preparing for the uncertainty-of-life and the end-of-life. Remember, our grieving process can be made more painful when we are faced with making all sorts of decisions that could have been handled by careful pre-planning.

Author's Profile

Thelma Manning Hall believes this "How To" Handbook Guide is "A Beacon of Light on Grief" for many stages and aspects of grief experiences.

It is a resourceful tool to provide information with template guides to help gather much needed information prior to end-of-life.

This book is intended to simplify complex processes when making arrangements for the living, the sick, and guide you through some legal requirements.

It is highly recommended for all family members, pastors, spiritual counselors, church leaders, funeral directors, doctors and lawyers.

It is one of its kind and at least one copy should be in every home.

The author has experience in a variety of professional and administrative fields.

Her professional experience as Vice President, Yandell Funeral Home, Webster Groves, Missouri, 1970; and as a Licensed Funeral Director, Layne Funeral Homes, 1979, attest to her experience in the industry.

Her administrative experience includes a variety of positions with the Pentecostal Assemblies of the World, Inc., including an elected position in 1967; and appointed positions as recording administrator for the Board of Bishops 1985-

1989; and concurrent Executive Administrator to the Convention Coordinator to 1997.

She is a graduate of California University of Theology and earned her Doctorate Degrees in the fields of Theology, Philosophy, Christian Grief Counseling and Administration.

The author is a graduate of Aenon Bible College, West Coast of the Pentecostal Assemblies of the World, Inc., and earned her Doctorate Degrees in Christian Administration Counseling, and Doctorate of Christian Grief Counseling.

She lives in North Las Vegas, Nevada with her husband and enjoys spending time with children, grandchildren, family and friends. She is married, mother, Christian, educator, consultant and speaker. You can reach the author at P. O. Box 336606, North Las Vegas, NV 89033 or authordrthelmamhall@gmail.com and https://twitter.com; www.Linkedin.com

Dedication

Family members
We Love and We Care

Our Present
To Plan in Advance Preparation for our Loved Ones

Our Past
Implementing that Preparation at End-of-Life

Our Future
Your Will, Your Estate Plans
As You Wanted

The Grief Process

Grief is a natural process experienced when we lose someone or something. Many of us have experienced loss, but want to know more about how to understand the grieving process.

It is the intent of this book to help educate and to help one learn the many facets and stages of grieving and to help one understand the emotions that happens whenever there is a loss.

It is important to know that God will help each of us work through our loss. It requires faith in God. Sometimes the loss of a loved one deepens our faith in God.

The definition of grief is: "The intense emotional suffering caused by a loss."

Grief affects how we feel and our state of mind. To mourn is to express those feelings. The path of grieving requires honesty.

There are stages of grief. There is a process of grieving associated with loss. These stages are important for us to know in order to help people go through what is referred to as a "normal grieving process."

The stages of grief do not occur in the same order for each person.

Granger E. Westberg book, *Good Grief*, talks about ten stages of grief.

These stages are:

1. **Shock** is a temporary escape;
2. **Emotional** is to release;

3. **Depression** is loneliness;
4. Physical **Distress** is despair;
5. **Panic** is fear;
6. **Guilt** is feelings of regret;
7. **Anger and resentment** is to place blame;
8. **Resistance** to getting back to normal;
9. **Hope** gradually returns to life again;
10. **Affirm Reality** is acceptance.

Again, the stages of grief do not happen in any particular order. Grief is a natural process. It is important to do everything possible to comfort and show compassion during the grieving process.

To mourn expresses feelings of loss and grief is a natural process that requires one to educate themselves in order to help others.

For further insight, read, *Through A Season of Grief,* by Bill Dunn and this book by Kathy Leonard, *Understanding Your Grief.*

Those who hope in the Lord will renew their strength.
They will soar on wings like eagles;
they will run and not grow weary,
they will walk and not be faint.

— Isaiah 40:31 (KJV)

It is necessary to believe God will help us get through our loss.

Funeral Etiquette

In looking closely at customs, traditions and expectations for the end-of-life services, the internet helped me to find this article.

While there is no universal guide to funeral etiquette, based upon many different cultures, religions and regionally specific funeral practices that take multiple forms, and a diverse population comprised of many demographics this allows many versions of funeral services.

Every family and every funeral service are different. How you dress in attendance to a funeral service is an indication of respect for the person who has passed away and their family. Do your best to adjust your actions, words and dress to accommodate these differences and this is half the battle.

Your manners and social graces are the most appropriate etiquette during a funeral service. There are many emotions, personalities and experiences expressed at a funeral service. If you are unsure of how to act at a funeral service, you can watch, listen and follow. There is usually a program and an individual tasked with leading the service and this will be your most valuable resource. Do your best to control your feelings and draw no attention to your inability to participate by being overly emotional. A show of respect and funeral etiquette is to leave your cell phone in the car or at the very least shut it off during the funeral service.

The visitation or viewing or a wake is a time prior to the funeral service where guests are invited to view the deceased person in the casket. It is customary to pay your respects by stepping up to the casket to view. If you are uncomfortable to view, focus your attention on providing comfort to bereaved members of the family and say, "I am sorry for your loss."

The family may or may not decide to have a graveside service. The funeral officiant will give further guidance at the conclusion of the service. You are not required to be a part of the processional to the cemetery.

A post-funeral gathering is sometimes held by the family and includes food and refreshments. Some friends close to the family will bring their contributions and sometimes the family will take care of the reception. It is important to remain respectful.

CHAPTER I

INDIVIDUALS

Ten Things Every Body Should Know

Decisions that Must Be Made

Advance Planning for End of Life

Ten Things Everyone Should Know
About Planning a Funeral or Cremation Service

By Dignity Memorial.com

While attending a bereavement ministry meeting, the titled pamphlet was discussed and my conclusion was this pamphlet would be helpful to anyone who is planning a funeral or a cremation service. No one wants to talk about death or dying, nor does one want to think about planning for their own funeral.

Reading this pamphlet will help you make informed decisions before the loss of a loved one. Upon the death of someone you care for, you want to make all the right decisions; especially when you have a limited amount of time to attend to all the details; and you want to follow all the steps required for a funeral service without feeling overwhelmed. Many decisions must be made when a family is grieving and when the family is not always prepared. Here are ten things everyone should know:

1 Be informed about the choices available. How would you like to be remembered? The funeral or cremation service should be personalized to reflect your wishes and should bring comfort to your family and friends. (See Part I)

2 Your wishes need to be documented. Many people think they have taken care of everything by writing a will, establishing a living will or even purchasing their cemetery plot. But that is not all. A will simply leave instructions for the handling of an individual's financial affairs, while a living will usually clarify certain general wishes regarding medical treatment. The funeral or cremation service still remains to be planned and paid for.

3 Talk about it with your family and incorporate their wishes. A funeral or memorial service is an import part of the grieving process. For family members and loved ones alike, the service provides an opportunity to express their grief, share memories, and to celebrate a life lived.

4 Decide the final disposition. Whether you choose traditional burial mausoleum entombment or interment in a cremation garden, determining your final disposition is a very personal decision, influenced by your faith and your beliefs.

5 Don't be afraid to ask about prices. The cost to arrange a funeral or cremation service can vary considerably from place to place. Be careful to choose a funeral home that presents its prices clearly and simply.

6 Consider planning and prepaying for your arrangements. Planning your funeral or cremation service in advance can take care of the details. But only prearranging (prepaying for your services) can take care of the actual expense of the funeral or take care of the actual expenses of the funeral or cremation service ahead of time, easing the future financial burden on your surviving loved ones. Your price is locked in when your rate is combined in pre-need funeral Insurance. Your choice of a cemetery, vault, open and closing of the grave, and the marker can be locked into your pre-need plan.

7 Why insurance may not be enough. Usually, life insurance, as well as final expense insurance provides a one-time lump sum benefit after a death has occurred. Sometimes there is fine print on the policy. It is important that you read your policy prior to the death of a loved one. If the person past one day after that age, the face value of that policy will not be paid by the company. Whole life (entire life) and the insurance company will have an age limit and Term insurance has an expiring age limit. There is no guarantee that the funds will not be consumed by a long illness or serious accident.

8 A prearranged funeral or cremation service and Medicaid assistance. If you plan to apply for Medicaid assistance, for yourself or a loved one, a prearranged funeral agreement can be extremely beneficial in meeting your needs. Consult with your attorney before applying for Medicaid assistance to learn more about your state's requirement. However, some states will have you declare your assets. Assets must be liquidated, especially if you have a home or assign your income to pay the facility for the care.

9 Find out ahead of time what Government benefits you are eligible to receive. Unfortunately, most funeral and burial benefits provided by the Social Security Administration as well as the Veterans Administration (V.A.) are limited. Most families find that additional funding is necessary in order to provide the type of funeral or cremation service they find appropriate for their loved one. To find out what benefits you are eligible to receive, contact Special Security Administration or visit their website at www.ssa.gov. For veteran's assistance contact the Veterans Administration office or go to www.cem.va.gov/benvba.htm.

10 Talk with your local memorial funeral and cremation provider. Arranging a funeral or cremation service can seem overwhelming and complicated, but there is always a provider close by who can help you.

Another informative Dignity publication, *At Your Time of Loss*, written by Alan D. Wolfelt, Ph.D., a noted author, teacher and practicing grief counselor known internationally for outstanding educational contributions to both adult and childhood grief. He serves as Director of the Center for Loss and Life Transition and is on the faculty at the University of Colorado medical School's Department of Family Medicine.

Decisions that Must Be Made

In a booklet, Personal Legacy, given to me from the Davis Funeral Home, Las Vegas, Nevada, there are 99 Decisions that must be made by a survivor after a death. By making these important decisions now, you can minimize the emotional strain that will be placed on your survivors.

The intent of this book, *A Beacon of Light on Grief*, will help families complete a separate plan on each individual family member. The asterisk (*) indicates details that can be planned, arranged and/or paid before the time of need.

A. **Secure Vital Statistics**:
   - ❑ Full name, complete address, telephone number*
   - ❑ Date of birth*
   - ❑ Place of birth*
   - ❑ Family Origin by Race: Caucasian, Hispanic, African American, Mullatto, Asian-American
   - ❑ Marital status* (Spouse maiden name)
   - ❑ International Citizenship (US/Canadian/Mexican) *(There are exceptions to the rule)

---

*Indicates details that can be planned, arranged and/or paid before the time of need.

❑ Optional (Father's birth place)

❑ Omitted Mother's maiden name

❑ Optional (Mother's birth place)

❑ Social Security number*

❑ Veteran's Branch of Service (DD-214) *

❑ Date & Place of Serviceman Data of Honorable Discharge*

❑ Optional (How long at current/former residence(s)

❑ Optional (Occupation, job title, nature of work & history*)

❑ Industry/location of work place, telephone number*

❑ Family origin*

B.   Pay Some or All of the Following

❑ Estate or inheritance taxes

❑ Funeral expenses*

❑ Permanent memorialization*

❑ Monument/Marker engraving charges*

❑ Funeral Director*

❑ Clergy*

❑ Organist and Vocalist*

❑ Florist*

❑ Obituary*

❑ Clothing*

❑ Long distance telephone or wire service

❑ Food* Reception or Repass (After the funeral service)

❑ Transportation or Limousine service

*Indicates details that can be planned, arranged and/or paid before the time of need.

- ❏ Doctors
- ❏ Nurses
- ❏ Ambulance, name, address, phone number
- ❏ Hospital, Nursing home, Group Homes, or hospice: Name, address, phone numbers needed)
- ❏ Medication & Drugs
- ❏ Current & Urgent bills (mortgage, rent, taxes, installment payments, utility bills, etc.)

C) Collection Documents and Paperwork

- ❏ Will (Check regarding special wishes) *
- ❏ Birth Certificate or Legal proof of age*
- ❏ Living Trust (check regarding special wishes) *
- ❏ Citizenship papers*
- ❏ Social Security Card or Number*
- ❏ Marriage license*
- ❏ Veteran's discharge certificate* or IRS Documents
- ❏ Insurance policies (life, health, accident, property, auto, etc) *
- ❏ Disability Claims*
- ❏ Bank books and listing of accounts*
- ❏ Other financial accounts*
- ❏ Property deeds*
- ❏ Cemetery deed or proof of ownership*
- ❏ Auto titles or bill of sale*
- ❏ Income tax returns, receipts & canceled checks*

*Indicates details that can be planned, arranged and/or paid before the time of need.

D) Decide and Arrange Within a Few Hours

- ☐ Exact location of interment*
- ☐ Location of service*
- ☐ Service type (religious, fraternal, military) *
- ☐ Time for visitation and funeral service*
- ☐ Arrange for special religious service*'(Picture for portrait, pictures for slide show)
- ☐ Provide information for eulogy*
- ☐ Casket (open or closed) *
- ☐ Outer Burial Container*
- ☐ Provide Vital Statistics about deceased for newspaper(s)* (Or just place of death notice (short) or the obituary (longer)
- ☐ Clothing and jewelry for deceased*
- ☐ Selection of scripture readings*
- ☐ Clergy to officiate*
- ☐ Funeral home preference*
- ☐ Marking of grave (temporary or permanent) *
- ☐ Charitable contributions for memorials in memory of deceased*
- ☐ Register book, memorial or prayer cards or folders*
- ☐ Select Pallbearers*
- ☐ Floral arrangements*
- ☐ Musical selections*
- ☐ Organist/Vocalist*
- ☐ Clothing for you and minor children*

*Indicates details that can be planned, arranged and/or paid before the time of need.

- ❑ Decide who will look after minor children or pets*
- ❑ House cleaning
- ❑ Extra chairs
- ❑ Transportation or Limousine for family & guest, including funeral procession lineup
- ❑ Reviewing and signing all paper work (Burial permit, interment agreement, etc.)
- ❑ Answering innumerable phone calls, messages, email, letters and wires
- ❑ Necessary meetings with funeral director, lawyer, clergy, cemetery, and sometimes with Social Security Administration.
- ❑ Arrange transportation & lodging for out of town guests
- ❑ Acknowledging those who helped in a special way (contributors of flowers, food, donations, babysitting, pet sitting. Order certified copies of death certificate* (Based on the number of Insurance Policies, Pensions, Bank Accounts)
- ❑ Food for family and guest*
- ❑ Items for memento display*

E) Plan to Notify as Soon as Possible

- ❑ All relatives
- ❑ All friends
- ❑ Funeral Director*
- ❑ Pallbearers*
- ❑ Cemetery*
- ❑ Doctor

---

*Indicates details that can be planned, arranged and/or paid before the time of need.

- ❑ Employer of deceased*
- ❑ Employers of relatives not going to work
- ❑ Organist, other musicians and vocalist*
- ❑ Newspapers regarding notices
- ❑ Social Security Administration*
- ❑ Veterans Administration*
- ❑ Insurance agents*
- ❑ Religious, fraternal, civic organizations & unions*
- ❑ Attorney. Accountant, financial planner & executor of estate*
- ❑ Attorney, Accountant, financial planner & executor of estate*
- ❑ Credit card companies*

---

*Indicates details that can be planned, arranged and/or paid before the time of need.

CHAPTER TWO

FAMILY INFORMATION

(INFORMATION TO GATHER PRIOR TO END-OF-LIFE)

SELECT FUNERAL HOME

VITAL DATA

FINANCIAL DATA

PERSONAL STATISTICS

MARTIAL DATA

PROFESSIONAL ACHIEVEMENT

RESERVE INTERMENT SPACE

CHECKLIST FOR FUNERAL SERVICE

FUNERAL NOTIFICATIONS

"How To" Plan Prior to a Funeral Service

("How To" Make Advance Preparations)

GATHER VITAL INFORMATION

(USE THIS TEMPLATE AS A GUIDE)

PART I. **Arranging for a Funeral Service**

(A family member should obtain this important information prior to arranging a funeral service)

Funeral Home Selection

Choose a funeral provider____

THE DECEASED INFORMATION AND LOCATIONS OF VITAL PAPERWORK

Social Security Card: ____

Birth Certificate:____

Marriage License: ____

Children's Birth Certificate(s): ____

Will Location: ____

Military Discharge____

Stocks____

Bonds ____

Mortgage ____

Deeds____

Bank Notes____

Automobile Title(s) ____________________________________

FINANCIAL DATA

Income Tax returns____________________________________

Valuables____

Other____

SAFE DEPOSIT BOX

Name of Bank____

Number____

Key____

BANK ACCOUNTS

❑ Checking

Name of Bank____

Location____

Phone____

❏ SAVINGS

Name of Bank____

Location____

Phone____

❏ CERTIFICATE OF DEPOSIT

Name of Bank____

Location____

Phone____

❏ INVESTMENTS

Certificate Number____

Location____

Phone____

❏ CREDIT CARD ACCOUNTS

Card 1, Type and Number______________________________________

Bank and Phone____

Card 2, Type and Number______________________________________

Bank and Phone____

Card 3, Type and Number______________________________________

Bank and Phone____

❑ REAL ESTATE OWNED

Property 1 Location____

Property 2 Location____

Property 3 Location____

Property 4 Location____

Property 5 Location____

❑ VALUABLE PERSONAL EFFECTS AND THEIR LOCATIONS

Item 1____

    Location____

Item 2____

    Location____

Item 3____

    Location____

Item 4____

    Location____

Item 5____

    Location____

Item 6____

    Location____

Item 7____

    Location____

PERSONAL STATISTICS

Name of deceased____

Address____

Years at present address __________

Previous address (if applicable) ____

Telephone___________________________________ Cell Phone_____________________

Date of birth_____/_____/_____

Place of Birth____

Social Security Number ____ ____ ____ - ____ ____ - ____ ____ ____ ____

Citizen of____

Naturalization Number________________________________ (if not born in U.S.)

Father's Full Name____

Mother's Full Name____

MARITAL STATUS

❑ Married ❑ Divorced ❑ Widower ❑ Single

Name of Current Wife ____

Name of Divorced Wife ____

Name of Divorced Wife ____

Name of Deceased Wife ____

EDUCATION

High School Attended____

Location____

From _____________ to___________

Secondary School(s) attended_______________________________________

From _____________ to___________

Degree (s)____

CIVIC ORGANIZATIONS

Public Office Held____

From _____________ to___________

Location____

Public Office Held____

From _____________ to___________

Location____

SPECIAL ACHIEVEMENTS

Award____

From _____________ To___________ Location__________________________

Award____

From _____________ To___________ Location__________________________

ORGANIZATION AFFILIATIONS:

Organization____

Office Held____ From ___________ To__________

Organization____

Office Held____ From ___________ To__________

Organization____

Office Held____ From ___________ To__________

BENEFITS DUE

Professional Statistics____

Company____

Location____

Job title____

Years worked: From ______________ To______________

MILITARY HISTORY

Branch____

Serial Number____

From ____________ To____________

Theater(s) of Service____ Grade______________________

Rank____ Rating_____________________

MILITARY (CONTINUED)

Citations____

Recognitions ____

Awards____

Membership in Veteran's Organizations_________________________

____

TYPE OF FUNERAL

❑ Traditional (with Casket)

❑ Memorial Service (Cremation)

❑ Combination Service (traditional service with cremation to follow)

❑ Urn

Type of Urn____

Memorial Instructions In Accordance with

❑ Will ❑ Trust

Name of Executor/Executrix_________________________________

Location____

Phone____

Preference in Burial Arrangements

❑ Ground ❑ Mausoleum ❑ Cremation ❑ Other ❑ Vault ❑ Casket

Cemetery____

Location____

Cemetery Section______________ Lot Number______________ Space Number______________

FuneralDirector____

Phone____

RESERVE INTERMENT SPACE IN MY FAMILY BURIAL PLOT

Name____

Relationship____

Cemetery____

Location____

TYPE OF SERVICE

❏ Church

    Address____

❏ Funeral Chapel

    Address____

❏ Graveside Service

    Address____

❏ Temple

    Address____

❑ Cemetery

Address____

❑ Chapel

Address____

❑ Home

Address____

❑ Other

Address____

Denomination____

Fraternal Organizations____

Military Organizations____

SPECIAL ARRANGEMENTS

❑ Scripture   ❑ Hymns   ❑ Flowers   ❑ Music   ❑ Pallbearers

PREFERENCE IN MEMORIALIZATION

❑   Bronze Memorial

Design____

Border____

Lettering____

Emblems or Inscription____

❑ Bronze Urn

Design____

Border____

Lettering____

Emblems or Inscription____

❑ Other

    Description____

CHECK LIST FOR FUNERAL SERVICE

❑ Make Funeral Plan   ❑ Make Funeral Service Arrangements   ❑ Choose Casket or Urn

CASH ADVANCE ITEMS

❑ Flowers   ❑ Death Certificates   ❑ Police Escort   ❑ Other

FINAL DISPOSITION

❑ Lawn   ❑ Crypt   ❑ Mausoleum   ❑ Niche   ❑ Other

❑ Outer Burial Container (Vault)   ❑ Interment

❑ Opening and Closing

❑ Monument   ❑ Memorial

DEATH CERTIFICATES (ORDER BASED ON NUMBER ENTITIES REQUESTING THEM)

❑ Life Insurance Policies   ❑ Pension(s)   ❑ Social Security   ❑ Other benefits

PART II. COORDINATING WITH CHURCH (IF APPLICABLE)

THINGS TO CONSIDER WHEN SELECTING A CHURCH

Does Church Have Templates for program: ❑ Yes   ❑ No

Does Church Have Template for writing an obituary: ❑ Yes   ❑ No

Date_________/_________/___________

Time____

Place for Service: ____

Coordinate Church Information with funeral director

PART III. FUNERAL NOTIFICATIONS

FUNERAL DETAILS

Place a death notice in the newspaper   ❑ Yes   ❑ No

Name of newspaper____

Address____

Phone Number or Email____

Online via social media   ❑ Yes   ❑ No

Contact family members   ❑ Yes   ❑ No

Close friends   ❑ Yes   ❑ No

Notify date_________/_________/___________   Time_________________

Location of Service: ____

FLORAL ARRANGEMENTS

❑ Casket Spray ❑ Corsages ❑ Boutonnières

Florist____

Address____

Phone Number:____

TRANSPORTATION

❑ Limousines

Number Needed________________

❑ Individual cars

Number Needed________________

FAMILY CLOTHING SPECIFICATIONS

Color coordinated: ❑   Yes   ❑No

CHAPTER III

Funeral Home or Mortuary Processes

Mortuary Process

Funeral Home

Coordinate with Church

Funeral Notifications

Mortuary Process

When a loved one has passed, the family member has to sign papers to select the desired funeral home to handle the funeral service. If the family member has a church home, the family member must notify the pastor of that church to coordinate the desired date of the service with the church and the funeral home.

Funeral and memorial services provide family and friends a place to express their feelings of grief and loss. It is not only a time to recognize a death, it is also a time to remember a life and recognize that your loved one has lived and influences many people during their lifetime.

The service is an extremely emotional time for the family. As bereavement ministry members, our function is to offer support, compassion, comfort and encouragement.

Services held at a mortuary chapel, the primary responsibility of their staff is to service the family. In contrast, the bereavement ministry of the church is responsible to support church members and their family with water and Kleenex.

FUNERAL HOME

PART I. FUNERAL SERVICE ARRANGEMENTS

Funeral Home Selection

Choose a funeral provider_______________________________________

The Decease Information to Give to the Funeral Director

Social Security Number: __ __ __ - __ __ - __ __ __ __

- ❏ Birth Certificate

- ❏ Marriage License

- ❏ Children's Birth Certificates

- ❏ Will

- ❏ Military Discharge Paperwork

Financial Data (Type of Payment)

❏ MasterCard ❏ Visa ❏ Discover ❏ American Express ❏ Bank Check

Name of Bank____

Card Number____

Expiration Date _______/_______ Security Code: _________

Personal Statistics

Name of deceased____

Address____

Personal Information

Years at present address _______________________________

Prior address (if applicable)____

Telephone____ Cell _______________________________________

 Date of birth___________

U.S. Citizen   ❑ Yes ❑ No

                   If no, Naturalization No_______________________________

Father's Full Name____

Mother's Full Name____

 Place of Birth____

Date of Birth_______/_______/___________

Marital Status

❑ Married ❑ Divorced ❑ Widower ❑ Single

Wife's Full Name____

Former Wife's Full Name (optional)______________________________________

Education

High School____

From __________ To__________

SecondarySchool____

From __________ To___________ Degree___________________________________

Civic Organizations

Organization 1____

  Office(s) Held_____________________________ From _________ To_________

Organization 2____

  Office(s) Held_____________________________ From _________ To_________

Organization 3____

  Office(s) Held_____________________________ From _________ To_________

Organization 4____

  Office(s) Held_____________________________ From _________ To_________

Public Office(s)

Position Held____

From _________ To_________ Location_______________________________

Position Held____

From _________ To_________ Location_______________________________

Special Achievements or Recognition

Achievement 1____

  From_________To_________Location_______________________________

Achievement 2____

  From_________To_________Location_______________________________

Profession

Position____

Company____ From __________ To_________

    Retirement Date ____/____/_______

Position____

Company____ From __________ To_________

    Retirement Date ____/____/_______

Military   Information

Branch___________________________________ Serial No_______________________________

From __________ To__________ Theater(s) of Service_________________________________

Grade___________________ Rank_______________________________ Rating_________________________

Citations____

Recognitions____

Awards____

Veteran's Organization Memberships:____

____

TYPE OF FUNERAL

❑ Traditional (casket)   ❑ Memorial (Cremation)   ❑ (Urn)

❑ Combination of Traditional Service (with cremation to follow)

MEMORIAL INSTRUCTIONS

❑ In Accordance with Will   ❑ In Accordance with Trust

Executor/Executrix____

Address____

Telephone_________________________________ Cell ______________________________

BURIAL ARRANGEMENT PREFERENCE

❑ Ground ❑ Mausoleum ❑ Cremation ❑ Other ❑ Vault ❑ Casket

Cemetery____

Address____

CemeterySection____

Lot Number_________________ Space Number____________________

FuneralDirector____

RESERVE INTERMENT SPACE IN MY FAMILY BURIAL PLOT

Name____

Relationship____

Cemetery____

TYPE OF SERVICE:

❑ Church ❑ Funeral Chapel ❑ Gravesite ❑ Temple ❑ Cemetery

❑ Chapel ❑ Home ❑ Other

Denomination____

Fraternal Organizations____

Military Organizations____

SPECIAL ARRANGEMENTS

❏ Scripture

 List Scriptures ____

❏ Hymns

 List Hymns ____

❏ Flowers

 Florist Preference ____

❏ Music

 Music Selections ____

❏ Pallbearers

 Names of Pallbearers _______________________________________

 ____

PREFERENCE IN MEMORIALIZATION

❏ Bronze Memorial

Design____

Border____

Lettering____

Emblems or Inscription_______________________________________

❑ Bronze Urn

Design____

CryptLetters____

Design____

CryptPlate____

Design____

Other ____

MAKE A CHECK LIST FOR FUNERAL SERVICE

❑ Make funeral plan   ❑ Funeral Service Arrangement   ❑ Choose Casket or Urn

CASH ADVANCE ITEMS

❑ Flowers   ❑ Death Certificates*   ❑ Police Escort   ❑ Other

*Death Certificates needed is based on number of: Life Insurance Policies, Pension(s), Other benefits that require proof of death.

FINAL DISPOSITION

❑ Lawn   ❑ Crypt   ❑ Mausoleum   ❑ Niche   ❑ Other

❑ Outer Burial Container (Vault)   ❑ Interment   ❑ Opening and Closing

❑ Monument   ❑ Memorial

PART II. COORDINATE WITH CHURCH (IF APPLICABLE)

Select a Church and Coordinate with Funeral Home

Does Church Have Templates for program ❑ Yes ❑ No

Does Church Have Template for writing an obituary ❑ Yes ❑ No

Date of Service______/______/__________ Time of Service ____________________

Place of Service____

PART III. FUNERAL NOTIFICATIONS FUNERAL DETAILS

Place a death notice in the newspaper ❑ Yes ❑ No

Online via social media ❑ Yes ❑ No

Contact family members ❑ Yes ❑ No

Contact close friends ❑ Yes ❑ No

Notify date______/______/__________ Time____________

SELECT FLORAL ARRANGEMENTS

❑ Casket Spray

❑ Corsages, number needed________________ ❑ Boutonnières, number needed________________

TRANSPORTATION

❑ Limousines, number needed______________ ❑ Individual cars, number needed______________

FAMILY DRESS

Color coordinated ❑ Yes ❑ No

CHAPTER IV

CHURCHES PROTOCOL TEMPLATES

(TO BE USED AS A GUIDE)

Church Ministry

Part I: First Call to Church

Part II: Decease Information

Part III: Membership Information (If Applicable)

Part IV: Funeral Arrangement

Part V: Information for Church Service

Part VI: Caterer Information

Part VII: Reception/Repast Information

The Church Ministry

During the grieving process, people often look to the church for guidance. The ministers are ambassadors for Jesus Christ and are vessels empowered by God to provide bereaved families with words of comfort, love, encouragement and guidance to help the bereaved through the process of losing a loved one.

Ministering to bereaved families require a gentle spirit, compassion, discernment and understanding even during this difficult time of loss. This can only be achieved through patience, prayer and the anointing of God. Following the Word of God, the minister shares biblical principles and this empowers the bereaved families with techniques to help them as they go through the grieving process.

The Word of God teaches:

God will never leave us nor forsake us. Hebrew 13:5 (KJV)

God will give the oil of joy for mourning and the garment of praise for the spirit of heaviness. Isaiah 61:3 (KJV)

Casting all your care upon him; for he careth for you. I Peter 5:7 (KJV)

And the peace of God which passeth all understanding, shall keep your hearts and minds through Christ Jesus and God promises love, and peace. Philippians 4:7 (KJV)

For God has not given us the spirit of fear; but of power, and of love, and of a sound mind. II Timothy 1:7 (KJV)

> Faith in God can encourage us to pray; For every one that asketh receiveth; and he that seeketh findeth; and to him that knocketh it shall be opened.
> Matthew 7:8 (KJV)

Only God can restore us to wholeness. This is the ultimate goal of the minister or the grief counselor.

FIRST CALL TO CHURCH

How to Handbook Guide to Help You Compile information upon receiving "The First Call" concerning the loss of a loved one. Be aware that each funeral service is different.

PART I — FIRST CALL

Date: _____________ Time: _____________ AM/PM   CASE #: _______________

Note: Upon receipt of first call, office staff shall notify the bereavement ministry or a designated point of contact.

Name of Caller: ____

Phone #: ________________________________ Cell: _______________________________

Primary Responsible Party: ____

Relationship: ______________________________________

Address: ____

City: ____ State: _________ Zip: _____________

Other Contact: ____

Phone #: ________________________________ Cell: _______________________________

Address: ____

City: ____ State: _________ Zip: _____________

How are you related to the deceased? _______________________________________

Are you the person responsible for decisions on behalf of the family?   ❑ Yes   ❑ No
   If no, request responsible person to call the Church with information concerning the deceased.

Are you the person responsible for payment of the funeral bill?   ❑ Yes   ❑ No
   If no, request responsible person to call the Church concerning financial arrangements.

PART II — DECEASED INFORMATION

Name of Deceased: ____

Addressed of Deceased: ____

Date of Death: _____/_____/_________ Place of Death: ___________________________

❑ Ship In____ (When your loved one is transported from another state to your state.)

❑ Ship Out (When you tell the mortuary you want your loved one to be transported to a mortuary in another state.)

Have you contacted a Funeral Home? ❑ Yes ❑ No

Name of Funeral Home: ____

Address of Funeral Home: ____

City____ State_______ Zip code____________

PART III — MEMBERSHIP INFORMATION

Was the deceased a member of church? ❑ Yes ❑ No

Are there extended family members of church? ❑ Yes ❑ No

   How many? _________________________________

If yes, Name of Family Member(s): ____

____

____

Address ____

City____ State_______ Zip code____________

Phone #: _________________________________ Cell: _______________________________

(Use separate sheet for additional names)

PART IV — FUNERAL INFORMATION

Note: Coordinate with church staff to clear date with master calendar of events before finalizing the dates with family or Funeral Home. Church staff will then follow up with the family or the Funeral Home to provide Church availability information and to help with making funeral arrangements.

Location of Services? ____

Alternate location: ____

When would you like to schedule the services? _________/__________/___________

Corporate Calendar availability Dates: _________/__________/___________

Funeral Home: Visitation: _____________ AM/PM Service: _____________ AM/PM

Date of Visitation:_________/__________/___________Date of service:_________/__________/___________Time: _____________

Officiating Minister: ____

Visiting Minister: ____ City/State _______________________________________

Note: Follow up by calling or meeting with the family at their home to obtain additional information, to show concern, to console and to pray with the family.

PART V — INFORMATION NEEDED FOR FUNERAL SERVICE:

What type of service are you considering? (Please Indicate)

❑ Traditional Service   ❑ Cremation   ❑ Memorial Service

Was the Deceased a Veteran?   ❑ Yes   ❑ No

Retired Veteran Requiring Gun Salute?   ❑ Yes   ❑ No

Name of Cemetery____

Location: ____

Has someone been designated for funeral arrangements/printing of obituary?   ❑ Yes ❑ No

Does the person creating the obituary program need an example?   ❑ Yes ❑ No

Note: Prior to printing, the church would like to proofread a copy of the completed program to include the obituary, pictures, video before printing the service.

Specify Number of Easels needed: ___________

Sanctuary Seating Arrangements:

Seating for family: __________   Number of rows to reserve: __________   Extended family: __________

Number of relatives in-town: __________   Number of relatives out of town: __________

PART VI — CATERING INFORMATION

(If a meal is to be delivered, provide this information)

Meal delivered to:

Name: ____ Phone: ____________________

Place: ____ Time: ____________________

PART VII — REPAST INFORMATION:

Note: It is the responsibility of the family to secure a facility for the repast.

Has the family secured a facility for repast?   ❑ Yes ❑ No

Do you want the repast information announced at the end of the service?   ❑ Yes ❑ No

CHAPTER FIVE

FUNERAL PROGRAMS

(Templates)

MEMORIAL PROGRAM

TRADITIONAL PROGRAM

OBITUARY

POEMS

Memorial Program Example

This should be helpful and should give you an outline from which to use as a guide. Below is a complete **Template Format** for **a Memorial Funeral Program**:

FRONT OF PROGRAM

The Information to include on the front of program includes:

- Full name

* Dates of birth and death

* Time, date and place of funeral

* Name of priest, minister or other dignitary officiating the service.

- Contact information such as a phone number or website address.

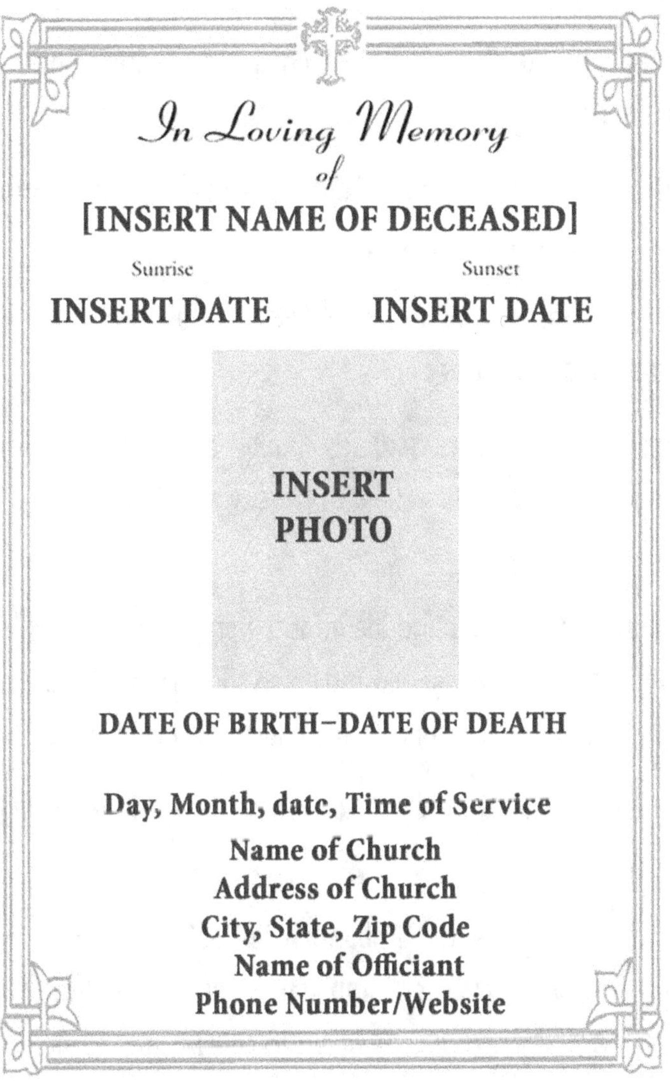

FIRST INSIDE PAGE OF MEMORIAL PROGRAM: OBITUARY

The section of the Memorial Program can include an obituary, life reflections, poetry or other things unique to the deceased. A template for some information you might want to include follows:

SAMPLE OBITUARY (CAN BE USED AS A TEMPLATE)

The Deceased was born on **[INSERT DATE]** to proud parents, **[FATHER'S FULL NAME]** and **[MOTHER'S FULL NAME].** in **[INSERT CITY AND STATE]**.

[DECEASED NAME] received his/her high school education at **[INSERT SCHOOL NAME]** From **[INSERT DATE RANGE]** in **[INSERT CITY AND STATE]**.

He/She attended **[Name of College or Secondary School]** From **[insert Date Range]** in**[INSERT CITY AND STATE]** and received a **[insert degree]**.

He/She was married to **[INSERT WIFE OR HUSBAND'S FULL NAME]** for **[INSERT NUMBER OF YEARS].** They have **[INSERT NUMBER OF CHILDREN]**.

[INSERT NAME OF DECEASED] was employed by **[INSERT EMPLOYER NAME]** and worked as a **[INSERT JOB TITLE OR DESCRIPTION OF JOB]**. He/She retired in **[INSERT RETIREMENT YEAR]**. (You may also include some information about his/her working life here.)

Final paragraph can include information about religious life, hobbies, memberships, club affiliations, etc. For example: Kenneth loved God and it was shown in his Christian walk with God. He had very strong faith in God. Spouse was a faithful member of Name Church. He loved his pastor and his church members.

The Lord called **[NAME OF DECEASED]** home on **[DAY, MONTH, YEAR]**. He/She answered in the quietness of his/her home.

He/She was a devoted Husband/Wife and Father/Mother: He will be remembered by **[INSERT CHILDREN'S NAMES, THEIR SPOUSE'S NAME, CITY AND STATE OF RESIDENCE]**, **[INSERT SIBLINGS' NAMES, CITY AND STATE OF RESIDENCE]**, **[NUMBER OF GRANDCHILDREN, NIECES, NEPHEWS COUSINS, ETC.]**, and **[NAME OF CHURCH FAMILY]**.

SECOND INSIDE PAGE OF MEMORIAL PROGRAM: ORDER OF SERVICE

Items to include in the order of service include, but are not restricted to:

- Processional
- Prayer
- Scripture
- Musical Selection/Solo
- Condolences
- Remarks
- Video
- Silent Reading of Obituary
- Eulogy
- Recessional

SAMPLE BACK PAGE

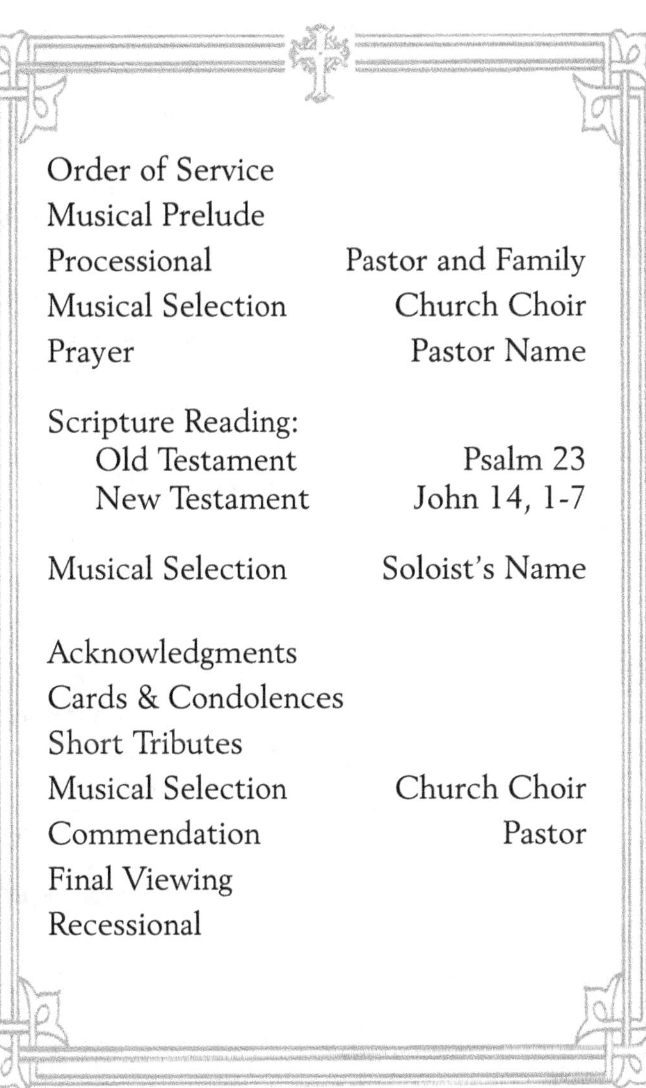

SAMPLE BACK PAGE OF MEMORIAL PROGRAM

Acknowledgment

[SAMPLE] *Perhaps you sang a lovely song,*
or sat quietly in a chair.
Perhaps you sent a flower or a plant,
if so we saw it there
Perhaps you spoke the kindest words,
as any friend could say
Perhaps you were not there at all,
just praying for us on this day
Whatever you did to console our family
We thank you so much, whatever the part.

A special thank you to **[INSERT PASTOR NAME]**, our
loving family members and many kind friends.

The Family of **[NAME OF DECEASED]**

Services entrusted to:
[INSERT MORTUARY NAME]
[INSERT MORTUARY ADDRESS]
[INSERT MORTUARY CITY, STATE AND ZIP CODE]

Interment: Private or Public

Repast **[INSERT LOCATION AND TIME]**

LAST PAGE OF TRADITIONAL PROGRAM (TO BE USED AS A GUIDE)

A traditional program has the same information on the front, but includes different information on the back, including:

- A more complete Acknowledgment
- Names of Pallbearers
- Names of Honorary Pallbearers

Acknowledgment

Insert Acknowledgment text

May God Bless Each Of You!
The Family

Active Pallbearers

Insert Names of Active Pallbearers

Honorary Pallbearers

**Insert Names of
Honorary Pallbearers**

Interment

Insert Interment Location

Will Those Driving In The Procession
Please Turn On Headlights For Safety.

Arrangements

**Insert Name of Funeral Home
Address, and Other
Pertinent Contact Information**

Obituary

(Template on "How To" write an obituary to be used as a guide)

An obituary is the synopsis of your life story.

1. Name of deceased person
2. When born, date
3. Place
4. Names of parents (State if preceded in death; as well as any sisters/brothers preceded in death)
5. Education
6. Organizations: Fraternities/Sororities/Eastern Star/Masons, etc.
7. Marriage(s)
8. Children born to the marriage(s)
9. Served in Armed Services
10. Work history
11. Religious Affiliation
12. Hobbies
13. Passed away (date) (place)
14. Leave to cherish memories — spouse, children, etc.

List family members, name, city, and state. Include this for parents, grandparents, husband/wife, sisters, brothers, aunt, uncles, nieces, nephews, cousins, god-daughter; god-son, extended family.

Selection of Poems

(To Be Used as a Guide for Choosing Poems for Funeral Programs)

Time Stood Still
Time stood still as the final sunset,
A hole was left in any heart where you were kept.

Sitting alone as I question why,
Wishing I had another opportunity to say good-bye.

Another chance to hear you laugh,
Another chance to see a smile on your face,
To open your arms for one more warm embrace, To sit and speak to you about
my day, I believed I had more time to say what I didn't say, The good memories
are there to aid me through,
To comfort me in those moments when I'm missing you,
You will forever be in my heart, so I'm never alone,
You're now at peace, you're finally home.

Rev 21:4 (NIV):

"He will wipe every tear from their eyes. There will be no more death or mourning
or crying or pain, for the old order of things has passed away."

Rev 21:4 (KJV):

And God shall wipe away all tears from their eyes: and there shall be no more
death neither sorrow, nor crying, neither shall there be any more pain, for the
former things are passed away.

Psalm 23

The LORD is my Shephard I shall not want.
He makest me to lie down in green pastures:
He leadeth me beside the still waters.
He restoreth my soul:
He leadeth me in the paths of righteousness
For his name's sake.
Yea, though I walk through the valley
Of the shadow of death,
I will fear no evil: for thou art with me; thy rod and thy staff they comfort me.
Thou preparest a table before me
In the presence of mine enemies:
Thou anointest my head with oil;
My cup runneth over.
Surely goodness and mercy shall follow me
All the days of my life:
And I will dwell in the house of the LORD forever.

Perhaps you sang a lovely song, or sat quietly in a chair.
Perhaps you sent flowers or a plant, if so we saw it there
Perhaps you spoke the kindest words, as any friend could say
Perhaps you were not there at all, just praying for us on this day
Whatever you did to console our family
We thank you so much, whatever the part.

Miss Me...But Let Me Go

When I come to the end of the road
And the sun has set for me,
I want no rites in a gloom-filled room.
Why cry for a soul set free?
Miss me a little, but not too long
And not with your head bowed low.
Remember the love that we once shared;
Miss me, but let me go.
For this is the journey that we all must take,
And each must go alone.
It's all a part of the Master's plan;
A step on the road to home.
Miss me, but let me go.
You are not forgotten, nor will you ever be.
As long as life and memory last,
We will remember thee.

Valuable Information for the Officiant
"How To" Template for Officiant

Officiant:

1. The role or duties of an officiator is to keep the program moving.
2. Stay within the time constraints of one hour to one and a half hours for entire program.
3. Keep remarks directed toward the occasions.
4. Add a comment every now and then; keep program moving.

Pray

1. Prayer on Funeral Program.
2. When programmed to pray: Pray for strength, comfort and encouragement during the family's time of grief.

Eulogy

1. To encourage the family with hope and inspiration.
2. Minister will preach to the living and those in attendance.
3. Minister will not direct words about the deceased.

CHAPTER SIX

TRADITIONAL CHURCH FUNERAL

PROTOCOL

FUNERAL DIRECTOR'S INSTRUCTIONS

HOLDING

ORDER OF LINEUP

PROCESSIONAL

DEPARTING VIEW

Funeral Director's Instructions for Traditional Church Funeral

The funeral director will contact the pastor of the church chosen by the family and obtain information as to designated area where the family will be seated. On the day of the funeral service, those instructions should be carried out.

The Funeral Director will set up procedures in accordance with Pastor's instructions. Upon arrival at the church, the bereavement ministry may can meet thirty minutes before the time of service to greet the funeral director and help with the lifting casket onto the truck and help carry in the flowers.

Funeral director will arrange the flowers at the altar. Nearest of kin or family members flowers are placed at the head of the casket and flowers from friends are placed at the foot of casket.

When family arrive at the church in a limo, the Funeral Director will lead Family into church. Some churches will have a holding area for the family prior to the start of the service.

Upon the start of the program, the line-up for the processional is as follows:

1. Pastor/Ministers
2. Funeral director

3. Family: Line up in twos with the person paying the bill first and nearest of kin to follow.

4. Seating position: Person paying the bill first seat; with nearest of kin to follow until all the family is seated.

   Optional: Based on instructions received from pastor, some churches will allow the funeral director to lead family into the sanctuary and seat family without a minister.

Visitation before the service starts: If viewing is before the funeral service, the casket is open until the service begins. Casket is closed during the service. Purpose of closing the casket during the service is to prevent people from going to the casket and disrupting the service.

Departing View: Church program will inform the audience. Funeral directors will follow the information on the program. *The funeral director will obtain information from the family if there will be a departing view.*

If there is a parting view, the funeral director will open casket, receive the pulpit ministers first, audience will be escorted from the last row to view their loved one proceeding from right of casket to view.

The funeral director will lead the family to view their loved one. Sometimes, the funeral director will attend to only the first row.

HOLDING AREA

The funeral director and the family, upon arrival at the church, will be assigned an area to wait until the funeral service is to start,

1. Have family gather in a designated holding area.
2. While in the holding area, the pastor will have prayer with the family.

ORDER OF LINE UP

3. The pastor will request family to line up in this order:
   a. Nearest of Kin
   b. Line up in pairs of two
   c. Proceed to enter sanctuary.

PROCESSIONAL

4. Protocol for entering the sanctuary:
   a. Pastor or Officiant leads family
   b. Reading scriptures: Division of Psalms 23, 25, 27
   c. Walk slowly until pastor reaches the designated seats reserved for the family.

FUNERAL DIRECTOR

5. Funeral Directors will:
   1. Seat Family on the left of casket (Traditional) or Urn (Memorial).
   2. Direct immediate family to seats on the first pew.
   3. All other family members will be seated in second pew and thereafter.

CHURCH DEPARTING VIEW PROTOCOL

At the conclusion of the Eulogy, the Funeral Director will come forward to prepare remains for the departing view.

Order of Viewing:

At the direction of the funeral director:

1. The ministers start the viewing process begin from foot of casket to head and may stand at head of the casket or as directed by pastor.

2. The right side of the Church - Ushers will continue to direct the congregants to walk around to the foot of the casket proceed to the head of the casket and return to their seats.

3. The left side of audience—Ushers will direct congregants by pew to walk around to the foot of the casket proceed to the head of the casket and return to their seats.

4. The Funeral Director will take the family around for viewing; the immediate family will be personally handled by the funeral director.

5. At the conclusion of immediate family viewing, the funeral director will call for the pallbearers.

6. The minister will lead the casket out of the church, one funeral director will follow in front of casket and the pallbearers will take their positions, three on each side of casket; the second funeral director will escort the family and follow behind the casket out of sanctuary.

7. Family members and guests who will drive to grave site, should proceed to their cars and turn their lights on if participating in funeral processional to grave site and instruct all drivers to obey the law and do not run red lights.

8. The Bereavement Ministry men will line up to remove funeral florals. Men will give vase or smaller plants to women. Men will carry the heavy floral pots or floral on easels.

CHAPTER SEVEN
HOSTING FUNERAL SERVICE

HOST CHURCH

HOSTING FUNERAL SERVICE FOR

GUEST CHURCH

ORDER OF SERVICE

Church Hosting Another Church
Funeral Service

When the family attends a small church and the expected attendance is greater than their church can accommodate, it is common to seek a larger church to host the funeral service.

Information Needed from Guest Church:
- Name of Deceased
- DOB
- Homegoing Date
- Homegoing Time
- Location
- Primary Party Contact Name
- Primary Party Contact Number
- Email
- Deceased Spouse N/A
- Type of Service (Traditional Funeral Service)

Funeral Home
- Funeral Home Contact
- Number of Guests

Requests

- No easels

Additional Information

- The deceased is not a veteran
- There will be a Parting View
- Program is due by Wednesday–submit by noon
- Advise family: The host church needs the name of the guest church, Name of Minister
- Guest Church will use host church program template.
- Family members may be on the program
- Guest Church may or may not use officiant of host church

Provide the Order of the Service to the Host Church

- Processional
- Prayer
- Scripture(s)
- Song(s)
- Condolences
- Remarks
- Slideshow (Video)
- Other Music Selections
- Eulogy
- Parting View
- Funeral Director
- Announcement: Location of Reception or Repast
- Recessional
- Funeral Director in Charge of the order for family departing sanctuary

- Encourages the family with hope and inspiration.
- Minister will preach to the living and those in attendance, and not so much about the deceased.

Program Template

- The family may participate on the program;
- Host Church or Guest Church may be the officiant
- Notify family Host Church request copy of program prior to printing program
- Host Church Bereavement Ministry Leader will assure smooth homegoing service.
- Officiant: Host Church Minister or Guest Minister

CHAPTER EIGHT

CHURCH BEREAVEMENT

(ALL MINISTRIES ATTEND FUNERAL SERVICE)

CHURCH BEREAVEMENT CHECK LIST

STANDARD OPERATING PROCEDURES

DRESS CODE

Church Bereavement Check List

Facility Director, Deacons, Safety Team, Ushers, Greeters, Ministers, Health Professionals, Operations, Production and Special Needs

All ministries are requested to serve scheduled funeral services. Every ministry includes the following:

1. **Podium** placed in lobby area for Memorial Registry sign-in Book.

2. **Memorial Service** — set up a <u>small</u> table to be placed in front of pulpit.

3. **Easels** — Pictures can be placed in the lobby or <u>to left of casket</u>.

4. **Video Taping** — Based on availability of staff and capability to reproduce, one copy to family.

5. **Video Presentations** — Limited to 2 to 5 minutes; family must notify staff to valid equipment capability.

6. **Programs** — Requested to be delivered prior to funeral service.

7. **Funeral Memorial Registry/Sign-In Book** — Placed on the podium <u>in the lobby</u> by Funeral Director.

8. **Flowers** — All floral deliveries to the church should be placed in <u>the front of the sanctuary</u>.

9. **Minister of Music** — All music requests from the family should be referred to music ministry for coordination.

10. **Deacons** — Assigned by Head Deacon and stationed at the front of the sanctuary to help persons up or down the stairs leading to the podium.

11. The **Facilities Operator** will check room temperature for room comfort whether air or heat.

12. The deacons will open doors of the church and the sanctuary.

13. The **Deacons** will arrive one hour or 30 minutes early to meet the Hearse, Limousines or individual family cars.

14. **Ushers** will arrive 30 minutes prior to service time and receive their positions or assigned stations.

15. **Greeters** will arrive 30 minutes prior to service time and receive their positions or assigned station.

16. **Ministers** will arrive 30 minutes prior to service time for prayer and designated seat assignments.

17. **Health Professions** will arrive 30 minutes prior to service time for prayer and designated seat assignment.

18. **Operations** will arrive 30 minutes prior to service time for special assignments from Head Deacon.

19. **Production** will arrive one hour to 30 minutes prior to service time to check the video/CD received from family member.

20. **Special Needs Ministry** will arrive 30 minutes prior to service time to accommodate family members or persons attending the service with disabilities.

Service Set Up
for Traditional Funeral Service

Duties of Bereavement Ministry Point Person and All Church Ministries

Standard Operating Procedures (SOP)

Bereavement Ministry Point Person or Facilitator

A.   Prior to day of funeral service:

1.   Call Family Member (provide information when needed, and have prayer with the family member)

2.   Call funeral home to obtain time remains will be delivered to church.

3.   Notify safety team — directs hearse to proper entrance.

B.   Call family to coordinate needs from the church:

1.   Music and/or Production Ministries (Video, DVD, CD).

2.   Information needed from family:

Obtain program, picture, DVD or CD, and memorial guest registry number of expected family members attending service, reserve seating by pew and number for total attendance to determine size of facility needed for service.

C.   Send out email notices to bereavement ministry members to determine how many members will be present to serve the family.

D.   The day of funeral service, facilitator will:

1.   Arrive at church one hour prior to funeral time.

2.   Coordinate with facility/operation person to obtain podium, easel.

3. Coordinate with facility staff to obtain bereavement ministry items – water, baskets, badges, Kleenex.

4. Coordinate with deacons concerning opening of doors for the arrival of hearse.

E. Facilitator performs other duties as needed:

1. Sign for and receive floral arrangements delivered to the church.

2. Arrange flowers with direction of funeral directors where to place flowers:

    a. Flowers from family are placed at the left of the casket.

    b. Flowers from friends are placed at the right of the casket.

Part I: As bereavement ministry coordinator/point person for church, will coordinate with all staff and ministries:

A. Bereavement Ministry members are requested to arrive 30 minutes prior to funeral service time.

B. Wear black suits and white blouses for women; black suits and white shirts and tie for men.

C. Have prayer with all staff present and assign positions.

Part II: Duties for each ministry at a traditional funeral service as follows:

Office Staff

A. Receives the call; a minister will follow up with the family.

B. Send information to Facilitator/Bereavement Coordinator.

C. Prepare the Condolence for the family's funeral service.

D. Proof read obituary received from the family.

E.   Prepare funeral program as needed.

F.   Obtain information for meal (Number of people, time and place of delivery).

G.   Send out information from Ministry Check List for each funeral service.

F.   Monitor and grant special request from the family.

The Church Facilities/Operations (building manager and his team):

A.   Will vacuum, dust, check bathrooms for paper towels.

B.   Will set up the sanctuary for the funeral service.

C.   Will check proper temperature of room.

D.   Will put Kleenex, baskets, water on the table for easy access.

E.   Will place easels, podiums in proper locations.

F.   Will perform other duties as assigned.

Deacons and Safety Team Ministry:

1.   The Church Coordinator will notify the Safety Team where to direct the driver of the hearse to the proper entrance.

2.   Deacons and the Safety Team will perform duties as necessary.

3.   Deacons and Safety Team will man the parking lot for safety of operations of funeral cars, line up of cars.

4.   Will place traffic cones for directing the traffic flow and/or parking.

5.   Will move around the campus property to detect suspicious persons and/or situations.

6.   Will ensure that all thermostats are set at 75 degrees.

7.   Will ensure that all TV Monitors and all Electronics are turned off (organ and keyboard)

8.   Will reset the alarm at end of funeral service if applicable.

Deacon Board (deacons)

A. The Deacons are assigned by the Head Deacon to attend the funeral service.

B. Deacons are assigned to help guest up and down stairs to the podium when program calls for making remarks.

C. The deacons' duties will vary as follows:

   1. Open the proper door; check and adjust room temperature of the sanctuary

   2. The deacons will direct the funeral cars to proper entrance.

   3. Open locked doors so the various ministries can get their supplies for a funeral service;

   4. Obtain podium, easels, etc., and place where necessary.

   5. The deacons will monitor the hall ways during the funeral service.

   6. The deacons will check the parking area, along with the deacon's helpers, when cars are arriving or departing.

   7. Will add folding chairs when attendance at a funeral service has an over-flow.

Bereavement Ministry:

A. Prior to the beginning of a funeral service, the Bereavement Ministry will prepare for the set-up of placing Kleenex, water and baskets in the first three (3) pews based on the number of family members.

B. One Bereavement Ministry member will be assigned to the Memorial Registry Sign-in book

C. The Bereavement Ministry will administer comfort to the family in a spirit of excellence by providing Kleenex, or removal of Kleenex from the hands of family members; provide water; escort a family member to the area of restrooms and escort them back to their seat. Provide information to family on an as needed basis.

D. Four to six Bereavement Ministry members are expected to be present at all funeral services. If the service is small, four to six members are requested to be present. If the funeral service is large, ten to twelve bereavement members are expected to be present.

E. One person is in charge and will make assignments; one person is responsible for members to sign-in, and will assign badges at the beginning of funeral service and collect badges at the end of a funeral service.

Greeters

A. The Bereavement Ministry Coordinator will assign the Greeters to a position in the absence of their ministry director.

B. Greeters Ministry will be assigned positions and will administer information, with a big smile, as guest arrive at funeral service.

C. Give guest direction to location of the main sanctuary.

D. Upon arrival, ask guest If you are a member of the family and direct the family member to the proper holding location.

E. If a funeral service attendance is small, a minimum of two greeters are requested to be present. If the funeral service attendance is large, a minimum of four greeters are requested to be present

NOTE: A good time for Greeters to leave their position is before the obituary is read.

Ushers

A. Ushers will be assigned to their position; one at the entrance door, and one positioned to seat the guests.

B. If the attendance for the funeral service is large at least four ushers will be required.

C. The Ushers will locate seats for the guests or order the seating of the audience i.e., assign special seating for ministries, like Deacons, Deacons' Wives, or Guest Psalmist.

D. Seating information is given to the Ushers upon their arrival and after the funeral service has begun.

E. The Process for Departing View: Ushers will have the section to the right will stand and beginning with the last pew follow the direction of the Ushers.

F. The Center Section will stand, proceed out to the Right and go around to the foot of the casket and return to their seats or leave the sanctuary.

NOTE: If the First Section is going down the Center Isle, the second section cannot go up the same isle. They must go to the Outer Isle and follow the flow of the people before them.

Ministers

A. The Ministers who are assigned to attend the funeral service, will arrive 30 minutes prior to the scheduled time of the funeral service;

B. Will have prayer with all their staff. The Ministers are assigned to a designated area.

Designated Areas:

1. When program participants arrive, they are assigned to a designated area.

2. NOTE: Pallbearers are usually seated together in a designated area.

Music Ministry:

A.   Based upon the family's request, a song will be provided.

B.   If family has no specific song, the Music Director will select an appropriate song.

C.   Music Director will select a psalmist to render selection(s).

D.   Make sure that all songs are appropriate for funeral services.

Production Ministry:

A.   Family must submit Video, DVD, CD limited to 3 to 5 minutes.

B.   Musician will play soft music prior to the start time of the funeral service.

C.   Will play the Video, DVD, CD received from the family.

D.   Will use internet technology to locate requested music when CD does not work on Church equipment.

E.   Will check the sound system.

F.   Will place microphone in proper position.

Health Professionals Ministry:

A.   Will come prepared to serve the bereaved family;

B.   Will be assigned to a designated position near the family.

C.   Will remain alert by keeping the family in their view.

D.   Will look for unusual body signs of stress.

Special Needs Ministry (Handicapped):

A.   Will be assigned to the first pew to the right section nearest to the entrance.

B.   A designated area will be set up to accommodate the Special Needs Ministry.

C. Will assist the Special Needs members with their individual needs, medication, water, restroom breaks, and provide diabetics with snacks.

NOTE: To avoid liability, at no time will the Special Needs Ministry administer medication.

Bereavement Ministry Dress Code

Remember, this is a ministry. Therefore, when attending the funeral service, the following dress code applies:

Women:

- Black suit and white blouse in Fall and Winter.
- Black skirt and white blouses, with long sleeves, in Spring and Summer.
- Comfortable shoes; no sports shoes.
- No pants.

Men:

- Black suit and white shirt, black tie in Fall and Winter.
- Black pants, white dress shirt, black tie in Spring and Summer.
- Comfortable shoes; no sports shoes.

CHAPTER NINE

Church Bereavement Ministry

SYNOPSIS

CREATE BEREAVEMENT MINISTRY

BEREAVEMENT MINISTRY DUTIES

LEADER QUALIFICATIONS

CONSOLE THE BEREAVED

MEMBERSHIP ROSTER

Synopsis Overview of Duties

The Bereavement Ministry serves the families of the congregation who have experienced the transition of a loved one. The bereavement process is not for the deceased; it is to help the grieving family. During the loss of a deceased family member, the Bereavement Ministry demonstrates four attributes: guidance, caring, comforting and consoling.

The Bereavement Ministry is familiar with helping the family through the funeral processes and will provide a basic template on the proper structure of an obituary template and the proper format template for a funeral program.

The Team Leader is notified of the date and time of On-Site funeral service. The Team Leader receives and provides information given on funeral service details to the Bereavement members and funeral directors.

The Bereavement Members are to:
1. Arrive 30 minutes prior to scheduled service
2. Set up sanctuary for Memorial or Traditional Service
3. Gather for prayer
4. Receive specific instructions
5. Distribute supplies (water, baskets, Kleenex)
6. Escort family members to holding area

7. Issue, remove, replace soiled Kleenex

8. Provide water

9. Meet and greet guest

10. Overseer Memorial Registry Sign In-Book

11. Receive Sympathy Cards

12. Distribute the Programs

13. Greet and seat guest as needed

14. Direct any problems to the Team Leader

Create a Church Bereavement Ministry

What Are the Duties of the Bereavement Ministry?

This grief handbook can be used as a guide to create a Bereavement Ministry Whether the church is small or large, the processes are the same.

Understanding the duties of the Bereavement Ministry will help ensure that care and attention are administered to each family based on their needs. The death of a loved one is an intense and painful experience for most people.

Having the right support during this time does make a difference. The church Bereavement Ministry is an excellent resource to work with families and to offer help to ease worry, stress, and anxiety. The Bereavement Ministry can help families cope with their loss.

The church could have a bereavement ministry dedicated to providing knowledgeable support to help the grieving families. Therefore, commitment to praying with the families and performing various duties can ensure care and attention is being shown as an act of love to the family. Each family has unique specifications.

The bereavement ministry provides an excellent service to families. It should be understood, upon consoling families, members of each family griefs differently.

Upon learning of the loss of a loved one, prayers are offered for the family during and after the service. Words of encouragement are carefully chosen. To fast and pray for the family helps to provide excellent service to all family members.

The members of the Bereavement Ministry may upon occasion accompany the families to the mortuary for "first viewing" of the loved one and accompany the family to "final interment". These are very critical moments for the family. One must be sensitive to the family and provide words of consolation. A family who is experiencing the grieving process does not always react the same. The Bereavement Ministry is committed to excellence.

During On-Site and Off-Site Funeral Services, Bereavement Ministry Members must be willing to serve:

- Attend scheduled services at their church to support bereave families.
- Attend services at another church to support members of their church who has lost a loved one.
- Attend services at the mortuary chapel to support members of their church.

Church Bereavement Ministry-Point Person's Duties and Responsibility:

A. Prior to day of funeral service:

1. **Call Family Member** (Provide information when needed, and have prayer with specified family member).
2. **Call Funeral Home** to obtain time remains will arrive at the church.
3. **Notify Deacons** to direct hearse to proper entrance of sanctuary.

B. **Call the Family** to determine their needs from the church.

1. Church needs to know if the family needs **music or the production ministries** to provide their services —Video, DVD, CD.
2. **Information Needed From Family:** Church needs to know from the family to obtain information for program; picture for easel; DVD, CD; and Memorial Registry Guest Book; number of family members attending funeral service.

C. **Send Out Email Notices to Bereavement Ministry Members** to determine how many members will be present to console the family.

D. The Day Of Funeral Service, Church Facilitator Will:

1. Arrives at the church one hour prior to the funeral time.
2. Coordinate with Church Facility/Operation Person to obtain podium,
3. **Coordinate with Church Facility Staff to obtain Bereavement Ministry supplies:** bottle water, small baskets, ministry badges, and Kleenex.

4. **Coordinate with Deacons Concerning Opening of Doors** for arrival of hearse directed to head into parking lot with door of hearse near the entrance of the facility.

5. Coordinator will **sign for and receive floral arrangements** sent to the church.

E. **Church Facilitator Performs** other duties as needed.

1. **Arrange Flowers with Permission of Funeral Directors**

   a. **Flowers from family** are placed at the **left** of casket.

   b. **Flowers from friends** are placed at the **right** of casket.

Duties of the Bereavement Ministry During Service:

1. Two bereavement members are assigned to stand at the second seat to attend to the need of the family, to comfort, remove soil Kleenex, provide water if needed. Bereavement Minister members are assigned attendants to take care of the family.

2. Assign a bereavement member as an attendant to receive guest and have them sign memorial registry book.

3. Receive the cards from friends of the family prior to entering the sanctuary.

4. Make sure there are plenty of Kleenex, and water available, as well as fans.

5. As a courtesy, escort family or guests of family to location of restrooms or water fountains

6. Bereavement Ministry members must interact well with others.

7. Bereavement Ministry facilitator will meet once a month to train the members.

8. When a Traditional Funeral Service is scheduled, the men will arrive 45 minutes early to help funeral directors, if applicable.

Church Bereavement Membership Roster

(Template Spreadsheet Format)

Day/Month/Year		
BEREAVEMENT MINISTRY ROSTER		
NAMES OF MEMBERS	**CELL PHONE NUMBERS**	**EMAIL ADDRESS**

Church Bereavement Ministry Leader

Conduct Meeting Template

- Start Promptly
- Identify Leader
- Begin with Prayer
- State Subject, Objective, Duration of meeting
- Review Agenda Topics
- Remain focused on the meeting agenda, objective, and schedule
- Record meeting results/open action items
- Get Commitments to Action Items
- Summarize Results of the Meeting
- Compliment Appropriate Results
- Announcements
- Benediction

Consoling the Bereaved

What We Should and Should Not Say

There are common clichés spoken to bereaved individuals that actually do more harm than good. Here are some suggestions to assist you when talking or writing to someone you are consoling during their time of loss:

DON'T: I know how you feel…

DO: I know you are hurting…

DON'T: At least he/she is out of his pain…

DO: Say nothing about the pain, just listen…

DON'T: You're still young; you can have another baby…

DO: Never suggest that a person could replace a baby (or even a pet)

DON'T: It was God's Will…

DO: God will comfort you… MATT 5:4

DON'T: Buck up; you have to be strong now…

DO: Trust in God for your strength. He'll supply everything you need to get you through each day, one day at a time. Just ask God and be specific. Say: "Lord, help me make the funeral arrangements," and "Lord, give me the strength to notify the family," etc.

DON'T: He/she wouldn't want you to cry…

DO: It is okay to cry. (Smile when saying this and offer a hug if appropriate.)

DON'T: Let me tell you what I went through…

DO: Leave your personal experience out of the conversation; if the bereaved asks about it, limit the discussion and put the focus back on him or her.

DON'T: If there's anything I can do, just let me know.

DO: Don't ask; just do it. A grieving person will rarely ask know…for help, but he/she will gladly accept it.

DON'T: It's been six months since he/she died, it's time to get on with your life…

DO: The amount of time a person takes to go through the grieving process is personal. There is no right or wrong amount of time to grieve.

DON'T: You should get rid of all his/her things. Having them around just keeps you sad…

DO: Again, the amount of time a person takes to grieve is different and is another individual's choice. Sometimes photos and personal belongings are pleasant reminders. Ask the Holy Spirit to guide you. If the person appears depressed or immobilized, you want to lovingly suggest counseling or other help.

DON'T: They went to sleep and the angels took them away. Never say this. Children may begin to fear sleeping to avoid facing the truth.

CHAPTER X
Doctors

Legal Checklist for Caregivers

Advance Medical Directive Template

(Medical Power of Attorney + Living Will)

Five Wishes and Hospice

Social Security

Veteran's Benefits

Safe Deposit Box

Legal Checklist for Caregivers

Tips on How to Protect Your Loved Ones and Yourself

If you are a caregiver, part of your job may be to keep track of your loved one's Legal affairs. You probably are learning, that it's a big responsibility.

"The ultimate goal is to make sure you have all the decision-making rights you need to manage your loved one's affairs," advises Charles Sabatino, director of the American Bar Association's Commission on Law and Aging. Here are his six tips on how to protect your relative's legal rights -- and your own.

1. Have the right documents

In addition to a will, make sure your loved one has a health care power of attorney (POA) as well as a power of attorney for financial decisions. These legal documents will allow an appointed person to make decisions for a frail or incapacitated relative.

Your loved one needs to create these documents when he or she is still capable to making decisions. It is not necessary to hire an attorney to draft a health care POA (though depending on your state, you may need two witnesses) . It is best to use a lawyer to draw up a financial power of attorney because money issues can be complicated.

The health care POA should spell out your loved one's wishes such as when life-sustaining treatment should be stopped (also known as a living will). You can find free advance directives forms and instructions on what to do in your state on the AARP Caregiving Resource Center.

See also the American Association website which has a **tool kit for health care planning.**

2. Make a family plan

Discuss these matters with all involved members of your family. Have your loved one put in writing who will be responsible for which caregiving role, and have all parties sign. This is not a legal document, but it will help keep peace with the family by making everyone's role clear. It is a fact, the biggest precursor of legal problems is bad communication.

3. Organize Important Papers

Most people don't realize how many legal documents they already have, or how many they will need for matters that arise. Important ones include birth and marriage certificates, divorce decrees, citizenship papers, death certificate of a spouse or parent, power of attorney, deeds to property and cemetery plots, veteran's discharge papers, insurance policies and pension benefits. Organize these document into files that are easy to navigate.

4. Explore Potential Financial Help

Investigate public benefits such as Social Security and Supplemental Security Income (SSI) disability programs, veteran's benefits, Supplemental Nutrition Assistance program (formerly known as food stamps), Medicare and Medicaid. AARP Foundation offers an online tool, Benefits QuickLINK, to help determine if your loved one qualified for 15 different government programs. The National Council on Aging offers a similar online tool called Benefits Checkup.

Also, examine your loved one's private disability or life insurance coverage, their pension benefits, long-term insurance and employee health insurance policy to see whether any of them cover home health visits, skilled nursing, physical therapy or any kind of short-term assistance that could include a mental health therapist or physical therapy.

If you take a leave of absence from your job to care for a loved one, you are entitled to three months paid leave under the Family and Medical Leave Act from your employer and are guaranteed your job when you return.

5. Think Beyond Your Loved One

If your parent is unable to take care of people who depended on him or her, you may need to take care of that role. This includes assuming responsibility for adult children with special needs. Make sure that child gets every available benefit, such as Social Security disability, local and state disability, special education programs and free transportation for the disabled. You may also need to assume oversight of benefits of the surviving spouse, too, by making sure the spouse is the beneficiary of your loved one's IRA, bank account, life insurance policy and pension benefits. Your loved one may also have a plan for pets in the will and money set aside to pay for their care.

6. Look for Tax Breaks and Life Insurance Deals

Keep all medical expense receipts for tax deductions. Your family member may claim federal deductions for many medical expenses including a hospital bed or wheelchair, out of pocket expenses not covered by health insurance (drug costs and Co-payments), remodeling the home to make it handicapped accessible and a respite caregiver to give the main caregiver a break.

Also, find out whether your family member has a life insurance policy that makes accelerated death payments to help pay for long-term care.

For a template of An Advance Directive Medical Power of Attorney + Living Will—Home(https://eforms.com).

Medical Power of Attorney
("How To" Template to be Used as a Guide)

STEP ONE: SELECT YOUR AGENT

STEP TWO: AGENTS DECISION

❑ I wish to accept all necessary treatment to keep me alive as long as possible.

❑ I wish to donate my organs

STEP THREE: ATTACH A LIVING WILL

This optional, although recommended, as a living will outlines your end of life treatment requests.

STEP FOUR: SIGN AND COMPLETE

Principal and agent must sign in accordance with their respective state's signing laws.

Also required are two witnesses or a notary public.

Provide a copy to physician(s).

Living Will

In a Living Will, you can define what you personally believe constitutes quality of life in order to inform medical professionals or family members as to what you would want to happen to you in the event of a life or death situation. Quality of life refers to your personal health and comfort standards in relation to a medical emergency or terminal illness.

Some states use the terms Living Will and Health Care Directive interchangeably, and some states use one term but not the other.

Without a Health Care Directive, the burden of making your medical decisions falls on your family members. Creating a personal directive not only gives you control of your medical wishes, but it saves your family from making tough treatment choices on your behalf.

The Living Will is an Advance Directive for Health Care. It is also a Durable power of Attorney for Health Care Decisions. It is an important legal document. It creates a curable power of attorney for Health care.

Before anyone signs this document, know these important facts:

1. It gives the person you designate as your agent the power to make health care decisions for you.

2. The person you designate in this document has a duty to act consistent with your desires as stated in this document or otherwise made known or if desires are unknown to act in your best interest.

3. Except as you otherwise specify in this document, the power of this person you designate to make health care decisions for you may include the power to consent to your doctor not giving treatment or stopping treatment which would keep you alive.

4. Unless you specify a shorter period in this document, this power will exist indefinitely from the date you execute this document and, if you are unable to make health care decisions for yourself.

My source: https://www.lawdepot.com.

Every state has its own limits as to what you are legally permitted to include in your directive. While you may specify instructions for a variety of medical situations and describe your feelings towards quality of life, keep in mind health care providers will only be allowed to carry out certain procedures according to your state laws.

Medical Power of Attorney Verses Living Will

Medical Power of Attorney:

A medical (health care) power of attorney allows an individual to give someone else the right to make decisions about their end of life treatment options.

Living Will:

A living will detail a person's end of life plans, in a concrete manner, without the useful surrogate to help guide medical staff as to their wishes. The instructions written are to be followed by the patient's primary core physician and cannot be changed by family or friends.

Check this source: https://eform.com for laws by state.

Advance Medical Directive

(Medical Power of Attorney + Living Will)

Information needed for an Advance Directive (Medical Power of Attorney + Living Will):

Who is this Power of Attorney for?

Name ____

Street Address _______________________________________

City ___________________________ State ______ Zip Code __________

Phone Number ____________________Cell Phone__________________

Signature____

Name of Person Acting on Your behalf ____________________________

Street Address _______________________________________

City ___________________________ State ______ Zip Code __________

Phone Number ____________________Cell Phone__________________

Signature____

2nd Alternate Agent

Powers ___________________________________State______End Date__________

Powers After Death ___________________________________

Living Will   ❑ Yes ❑ No Organ Donation ❑ Yes ❑ No

Power of Attorney Location __________________________________

Primary Care Physician ______________________________________

Execution ____

Five Wishes

(Ask your doctor for a Copy of the Five Wishes Booklet—Health Care Partners)

It was while attending a Bereavement Ministry meeting that I first learned about the Five Wishes, and would suggest you ask your doctor if your clinic has can obtain the booklet titled, "Five Wishes, from Health Care Partners, A DaVita Medical Group. This is the first living will that talks about our personal, emotional and spiritual needs, as well as our medical wishes. It lets you choose the person you want to make health care decisions for you if you are not able to make them for yourself.

Five Wishes will let you say exactly how you wish to be treated if you get seriously ill. It is your medical directive.

It was written with the help of the American Bar Association's Commission on Law and Aging, and the nation's leading experts in end-of-life care. It is also easy to use.

Five Wishes began 12 years ago when Jim Towey, who worked closely with Mother Teresa. He lived in a hospice she ran in Washington, DC for one year.

Five Wishes

Inspired by this first-hand experience, Mr. Towey sought a way for patients and their families to plan ahead and to cope with serious illness. The result is *Five Wishes* and the response to it has been overwhelming. It has been featured on CNN and NBC's Today Show and in the pages of Time and Money magazines. Newspapers have called *Five Wishes* the first "Living will with a heart and soul." Today, *Five Wishes* is available in 23 languages.

There are many things in life that are out of our hands. This "Five Wishes" booklet gives you a way to control something very important — how you are treated if you become seriously ill. It is an easy-to-complete form that lets you say exactly what you want. Once it is filled out and properly signed it is valid under the laws of most states.

How Five Wishes Can Help You and Your Family

1. It lets you talk with your family, friends and doctor about how you want to be treated if you become seriously ill.

2. Your family members will not have to guess what you want. It protects them if you become seriously ill, because they won't have to make hard choices without knowing your wishes.

3. You can know what your mom, dad, spouse, or friend wants. You can be there for them when they need you most. You will understand what they really want.

This booklet guides individuals to state their wishes in these five important decision-making areas of your life:

1. The Person I Want to Make Care Decisions for Me When I Can't.
2. The Kind of Medical Treatment I want or Don't Want.
3. How Comfortable I Want to Be.
4. How I Want People to Treat Me.
5. What I Want My Loved Ones to Know.

"We all have the power to make a real difference in our own care or that of a loved one." People may think of Hospice as a place. It is not. It is a service. Family Home Hospice has offered medical services and emotional support when care shifts from treatment for a cure, to pain management and maximum comfort. It is all about quality of life, and Family Home Hospice makes every moment count. A complete team could consist of experienced registered nurses, social workers, therapists, home health aides, pastoral counselors, and trained volunteers that provided fully integrated care to patients and families during the end stages of life.

Social Security

(To be used as a "How To" Template)

There are so many facets of life that remains to be completed after the death of a loved one. The emotional and cognitive effects when a grieving person feels least able to handle extra pressure.

There is usually an increase in things that have to be done including, paying extra bills connected with funeral and hospital expenses; meeting with lawyers concerning the deceased person's will, trust and living will, submission of filing insurance, and Social Security.

Social Security is a form of insurance that plays a very important part in estate planning. Most of us are entitled to some form of these benefits. But it is important to realize that Social Security Benefits are not paid automatically.

You must apply for these benefits on special forms, and certain documents must be furnished at that time and within a certain time limit.

Here is a list of documents you will need:

1. Social Security with proof of death (Copy of Death Certificate);

2. Social Security Card for the deceased;

3. Copy of marriage certificate;

4. Birth Certificate of Applicant;

5. Birth Certificate of Deceased;

6. Birth Certificate of minor children;

7. Disability Proof for children over 18; and

8. Proof of support if applicant is parent or husband.

Death Benefits: A lump sum will be made to the surviving spouse if he or she was living in the same household with the insured person at the time of death. If no qualified spouse survives, the payment can be made only to eligible children.

Survivor's payment: If an insured person dies, the widow, dependent widower, children and dependents parents of that person my be eligible for monthly survivor's payments. For additional information visit your Social Security Office.

Veteran's Benefits

(To be used as a "How To" Template)

Veterans' survivors are entitled to many burial related benefits. However, these will not be paid automatically. Claims for Veterans' benefits must usually be made within two years from the date of final interment.

As an honorably discharged veteran from the air Force, Army, Navy, Marines, or Coast Guard, you are entitled to:

1. A burial allowance limited to $300 for expenses for burial and funeral of deceased. This allowance will be paid only for veterans who were entitled to receive a VeteransAdministration pension or compensation.

2. An allowance of $150 payable towards the burial plot expenses of a Veteran who is *not* buried in a National cemetery.

3. A burial flag, that can be given to next of kin or friend of deceased.

4. Bronze Memorial or headstone.

Veterans' benefits are frequently altered and revised. There may also be Veterans benefits from your county. To determine your eligibility or to file your claim, contact your local Veterans Administration, Washington, D.C. 20421.

To File a Claim for Veteran's Benefits:

The following forms must be submitted:

1. Need Veteran's Discharge papers, DD 214)

2. Certified copy of Death Certificate

3. Copy of Marriage Certificate

4. Birth Certificate of minor children

5. Receipted itemized funeral bill

Safe Deposit Box

(To be used as a "How To" Template)

After a death, the safe deposit box is usually sealed and cannot be opened unless the executor or administrator of the estate has been appointed or in the presence of an Inheritance Tax Department representative.

A safe-deposit box at a local bank or credit union may be the best place to store hard-to-replace documents, jewelry and other small valuables. But it could be the worst place for certain other items.

Here is a quick run-down of what to keep in —and keep out — your safe-deposit box:

1. Only copy of your will.

2. Valuables you haven't inventoried.

3. Cash.

Put these in:

4. An inventory of your household possessions

5. Your passport.

6. Deeds and titles

7. The originals of your birth certificate and marriage license.

8. Stock and bond certificates and U.S. Savings bonds.

9. Valuable jewelry you rarely wear.

There are so many facets of life that remain to be completed after the death of a loved one. This is when you are least able to handle the emotional pressure. There is usually such an increase of things that have to be done including, paying extra bills connected with funeral and hospital expenses, meeting with lawyers concerning deceased person's will, trust and living will, submission of filing insurance, social security and veteran department claims, putting the utility bill into your name, changing the lease agreement, consolidating and name changes on bank and pension statements, changing names on legal documents and the list goes on and on. There are templates to guide you through some of these processes.

Life goes on and the processes involved are endless depending on your lifestyle.

Bereavement can be stressful and bad on your health, and on your body. Grief can leave you with a feeling of inner emptiness, guilt, anger, irritability, and withdrawal from others, forgetfulness, loneliness, and error in judgment. Grief can interfere with the body and its immune system; and can have physical negative effects on your health.

One of the most difficult grieving experiences is the loss of a child. My experience was with a mother who lost one of her twin sons. Her heart was broken and so heavy with grief. All she could say is, "My son is gone."

Her doctor gave her pills to quiet the pain and to help her cope with the pain she was experiencing over the loss of her son. Never the less, the tears would not stop flowing. Death is final. Coming to grips with that reality is most difficult.

CHAPTER ELEVEN

LAWYERS

POWER OF ATTORNEY HELP GUIDE (FINANCIAL & LEGAL)

(Templates)

ESTATE PLANNING

FINANCIAL INFORMATION

IMPORTANCE OF A WILL

WILLS & TRUSTS

REVOCABLE & IRREVOCABLE TRUSTS

ESTATE PLANNING VALUE CALCULATED

Power of Attorney Help Guide

Completing Your Document

In Legal Nature's **power of attorney,** you, the principal, will specify what **powers your "agent"** (aka your attorney-in-fact) has. You can give your agent decision-making authority over almost any of your affairs, and our power of attorney form gives you complete flexibility in tailoring the document to your specific needs.

Power of Attorney

Note, however, that some powers cannot legally be delegated to your agent, including the powers to make, **amend**, or revoke your **will;** to change insurance beneficiaries; and to vote in a public election.

A general power of attorney **terminates when you die or become incapacitated.** However, a durable power of attorney allows your agent to act for you even when you become incapacitated. "Incapacitated" means that you are no longer able to understand and evaluate information in order to make competent decisions regarding your affairs, usually due to physical or mental impairment. A **durable power of attorney** continues until you die or revoke your agent's powers.

Choosing Your Agent

An agent can be a friend, family member, business partner, or anyone else you trust. Your **agent** will also be entitled to receive reasonable compensation for the work they perform unless you specify otherwise.

Executing Your Document

To make your power of attorney legally binding, you need to sign the document in the presence of the appropriate witnesses. Check your state's witnessing requirements. As financial institutions and other entities often require it to be notarized. It is recommended that you use a notary even if your State does not require it. Make sure any witnesses you use are not appointed as agents in the instrument, related to the principal by blood or beneficiaries of the principals.

You do not have to record a power of attorney to make it legally binding. However, if you are giving your agent the power to handle real estate transactions for you, and it is likely your agent will use this power on your behalf in the future is best to go ahead and record the document for a small fee (usually $20-$30).

Remember you can amend or revoke your power of attorney at any time after it goes into effect.

Power of Attorney Checklist

Step 1: Communicate Your Wishes

It is recommended that you discuss your power of attorney with your agent and any other named in the document. This could include one or more named guardians or physicians. Doing so will help ensure that your wishes are clearly communicated and understood at the time of signing.

Step 2: Review and Sign

Next, review your document and make any final changes or clarifications. Follow your state's witnessing requirements when signing, which are included with the instructions. Most states require either a notary or two disinterested persons to witness the principal sign.

Step 3: Distribute Copies

All parties named in the document should receive a copy of the power of attorney once it is fully executed.

Step 4: Periodically Review and Update

The principal will need to review the document and make any needed updates at least every couple of years. Life events often cause the principal's needs and wishes to change over time. Legal Nature's power of attorney will automatically revoke your original power of attorney while allowing you to update your wishes.

Step 5: Revoke Your Agent's Authority (Optional)

In the event that you wish to terminate the agent's authority to act on your behalf, you need to complete a revocation of power of attorney form. However, if you simply wish to change or add agents, then you should create a new power of attorney.

ESTATE INFORMATION

(Use as a "How To" Template)

I have a Will ☐ Yes ☐ No Date of Will _______/_______/___________

Location of Will ☐ At Home ☐ Attorney's Office Other_______________________________________

Name of Attorney_______________________________________

Address _______________________________________

City_______________________________________State___________Zip Code____________

Office Phone _______________________________Cell Phone _______________________________

Email _______________________________________Other_______________________________

Name of Executor/Executrix_______________________________________

Address _______________________________________

City_______________________________________State___________Zip Code____________

Phone_______________________________________Cell Phone _______________________________

Email _______________________________________Other_______________________________

Prepared By

Name_______________________________________

Address _______________________________________

City_______________________________________State___________Zip Code____________

Phone_______________________________________Cell Phone _______________________________

Email _______________________________________Other_______________________________

FINANCIAL INFORMATION

BANKING

Bank Name _________________________________ Branch _________________________________

Type of Account ❑ Checking   ❑ Savings

Checking Account #_________________________________or Savings #_________________________________

Online Account Information: Username _________________________________Password _________________________________

CERTIFICATE OF DEPOSIT

Bank Name _________________________________ Branch _________________________________

Online Account Information: Username _________________________________Password _________________________________

INVESTMENTS

Bank Name _________________________________ Branch _________________________________

List Investments_________________________________

Certificate Number_________________________ Location_________________________________

CREDIT CARDS

❑ Visa   ❑ Master Card   ❑ Am Express   ❑ Discover   ❑ Other_________________________________

Card Number_________________________________Expiration _____/_____Security Code__________

Online Account Information: Username _________________________________Password _________________________________

❑ Visa   ❑ Master Card   ❑ Am Express   ❑ Discover   ❑ Other_________________________________

Card Number_________________________________Expiration _____/_____Security Code__________

Online Account Information: Username _________________________________Password _________________________________

CREDIT CARDS (CONTINUED)

❑ Visa ❑ Master Card ❑ Am Express ❑ Discover ❑ Other_______________________

Card Number______________________________Expiration _____/_____Security Code__________

Online Account Information: Username _______________________________Password _______________

❑ Visa ❑ Master Card ❑ Am Express ❑ Discover ❑ Other_______________________

Card Number______________________________Expiration _____/_____Security Code__________

Online Account Information: Username _______________________________Password _______________

❑ Visa ❑ Master Card ❑ Am Express ❑ Discover ❑ Other_______________________

Card Number______________________________Expiration _____/_____Security Code__________

Online Account Information: Username _______________________________Password _______________

❑ Visa ❑ Master Card ❑ Am Express ❑ Discover ❑ Other_______________________

Card Number______________________________Expiration _____/_____Security Code__________

Online Account Information: Username _______________________________Password _______________

Estate Information
(Use as a "How To" Template)

Importance of a Will

If you die without a Will, state law and the courts may determine who will administer your estate, handle financial matters and act as guardian for your minor children, but with a Will, you decide.

In some instances, joint ownership of property may not be a good substitute for a carefully drafted Will. For instance, you and your spouse died as a result of a common accident, before the survivor had an opportunity to execute a proper Will, your property would pass to whomever or whatever in accordance with state law.

You should review your Will every few years, particularly if you have moved or your family situation has changed since you last executed a Will. State laws vary as to formal requirements and as to the rights of children and grandchildren born after a Will was executed.

When you realize how much is at stake, the well-being of your entire family and the protection of your property, we believe that you will find that the attorney's fee for drafting your Will and planning your estate is a worthwhile investment.

However, a Trust will be stronger than a Will because in some cases the Trust will avoid Probate.

Wills

(To be used as a "How To" Template)

Everyone needs a will. A will is one of the finest protections you can give to those special people in your life…a husband or wife, children, relatives, good friends or special charity. To avoid probate, you will also need a Living Trust.

An up-to-date will is the only way that you can control the distribution of your property at death. Otherwise, the state takes over and your property is distributed according to established laws of succession. Your lawyer will help you write your will tailored to your exact wishes. If you have not made your will, you should do so as soon as possible. (https://formswift.com/builder.php?documentType_last-will-and-testament)

What Is a last will and testament? A last will and testament is a legal document that details how a person's assets and properties will be distributed after their death. The legal document can also detail custody and guardianship details for the surviving children if necessary. Since today's world also has many technological aspects, digital assets can now also be included in a last will and testament.

When completing a last will and testament, you will need to have a clear idea about what you want to happen to your financial and real estate assets. You should have personal information for the party's that will be receiving these assets in the event of your death. If you have the information you need, you can create a will without the assistance of a lawyer. (https://formswift.com/builder. php?documentType=last-and-testament) Get started now!

Will and Trust Items to Keep Track Of

You've gone to the necessary trouble of drawing up your will and perhaps creating a trust. Now you need to make a list of the locations of important papers and make sure that you and at least one other trusted person know where the list is and where the locations are. Include the locations of the following items:

- Your will

- Your trust(s)

- Your healthcare proxy

- Your living will

- Your tax records

- Your safe deposit box

People Who Can Help with Your Estate Plan

The professionals who help you set up your will and trusts can be useful not only during the creation of these documents, but also later on if you want to make changes. They can be invaluable resources for your executor and loved ones when the time comes. Keep a list of the names, addresses, and phone numbers of the following professionals:

- Your personal representative

- Your trustee

- The guardian for your children

- Your attorney-in-fact

- Your healthcare advocate

- Your estate planning lawyer

When to Review Your Estate Plan

You should review your estate plan, including your will and any trusts, on a periodic basis to be sure that your inheritance planning is consistent with your needs and goals. In addition, review your estate plan upon:

- Marriage, separation or divorce

- Birth or adoption of a child

- Death of an heir

- Move to another state

- Significant changes in your health

- Significant changes in your financial condition

How to Prepare for a Meeting with an Estate Planning Lawyer

You want your will and trust to be legal, so it makes sense to meet with a lawyer to form your estate plan. Lawyers who specialize in estate planning can help you cover all contingencies and help make sure that your plan is complete. Use the tips in the following list to prepare for your meeting:

- Ask about your lawyer's experience. You'll benefit if your lawyer has worked with estates similar to yours.

- Before you meet an estate planning lawyer, most law offices will provide you with a questionnaire to complete and a list of documents to take with you to your meeting. You will save time and possibly money by completing the questionnaire and compiling the documents before your consultation.

- Be clear on what estate planning documents are included in your estate plan and what your lawyer will charge to complete those documents. Get an estimate of how much your complete estate plan will cost.

- Discuss estate taxes with your lawyer. Estate tax law is in a state of flux. Your lawyer can help you figure out whether your estate is likely to have to pay estate taxes and, if so, how to minimize or avoid them.

- Discuss any special circumstances with your lawyer. Do you have a family business? An heir with a disability? Children from a prior marriage or relationship? Your lawyer needs to know your needs in order to plan your estate.

How to Plan for Incapacity in Your Will and Trust

It's not easy to think about, but your will and trust(s) need to include provisions that go into effect if you become incapacitated for any reason. Your executor and your heirs will be grateful for your forethought. Keep in mind the following points about planning for incapacity:

- If you don't create a plan for your incapacity, a court may appoint somebody to oversee your personal and financial needs. By planning for incapacity, you can choose the people who will help you, provide them with guidance as to your wishes, impose limits on their powers, or grant them powers beyond what a court may allow.

- Your durable power of attorney designates the person who can assist you with your financial affairs or manage them on your behalf.

- Your healthcare proxy appoints the person who will assist you with decisions concerning your medical care or make those decisions for you consistent with your instructions.

- You can provide within your living trust for your trustee to gain immediately authority over your trust assets if you become incapacitated.

- Your living will provide guidance to your family and doctors as to the type of treatment you want during the final days of your life.

Revocable Trust Versus Irrevocable Trust?

Estate planning, as explained by N. Brian Caverly and Jordan S, Simon in Estate Planning for Dummies, often involves setting up a revocable trust or irrevocable trust. Each one of those trusts begins with an inter-vivos trust — a trust you set up that goes into effect while you are still alive.

You then decide if the inter-vivos trust is revocable, meaning that you can change your mind, or irrevocable, meaning sorry, what's done is done.

Irrevocable trusts are the easier of the two to understand. After you place property into an irrevocable trust, you cannot retrieve the property. For all intents and purposes, that property now belongs to the trust, not to you.

With a revocable trust, you can place property into the trust and at some point in the future, undo the transfer by removing the property and terminating the trust.

Very often, if you die or become incompetent, the provisions of a revocable trust call for the trust to become an irrevocable trust. For example, you can terminate a revocable burial trust at any time, usually before death or incompetency. But if the burial trust still exists when you die or become incompetent, the trust becomes irrevocable and the money is used for your burial expenses.

You most likely have a gift tax consequence when you establish an inter-vivos irrevocable trust, so make sure your accountant is "in the loop," along with your attorney. Also, certain transfers within certain time periods prior to your death can be included in your estate as "gifts in contemplation of death" under both state and federal statutes. So, watch out for possible death tax implications!

How Revocable and Irrevocable Trusts Affect Estate Taxes

The most significant distinctions between revocable and irrevocable trusts are the estate tax considerations. Property that you place in an irrevocable trust is no longer considered part of our estate, meaning that the property typically is not included in our estate's value when it comes to determining if you owe death taxes and, if so, how much.

However, you still own property that you place into a revocable trust, and, therefore, that property is still subject to death taxes. If you can change your mind about the trust and retrieve the property from the trust at any time while you are still alive, the property is really yours and should be considered part of your estate.

So, if you only get a break on estate taxes with an irrevocable trust, why would anyone want to use a revocable trust without the estate tax break? Estate tax savings is only one of the reasons you may consider including a trust in your estate planning.

Calculating the Value of Everything You Own for Estate Planning

By N. Brian Caverly, Jordan S. Simon

Before you can plan how to distribute your assets after your death, you need to understand what your estate is. In the most casual sense, your estate is your stuff or all your possessions. In addition to understanding what your estate is, you also need to know what your estate is worth. First you make a list of positive balance items such as:

- Cash, checking and savings accounts

- Certificates of deposit (CDs)

- Stocks, bonds, and mutual funds

- Retirement savings in your Individual Retirement Account (IRA), 401(k), and other special accounts

- Household furniture (including antiques)

- Clothes

- Vehicles

- Life insurance

- Annuities

- Business interests

- Jewelry, baseball card collection, autographed first edition of *Catcher in the Rye*, etc.

You calculate your estate's value as follows:

Add up the value of all of the positive balance items in your estate. What's that, you say? You don't own a house or any other real estate, so you think that you don't have an estate? Not so fast! In a legal sense, all kinds of items are considered to be your property.

Subtract the total value of all of the negative balance items, such as the outstanding balance of the mortgage you owe on your house or a vacation home, the outstanding balances on your credit card accounts, taxes you owe to the government, or any IOUs to people that you haven't paid off yet

Determining your estate's value can be more complicated than creating two columns on a sheet of paper or in your computer's spreadsheet program and doing basic arithmetic. If you are a farmer, for example, you need to figure out the value of your crops or livestock. If you own a small one-person business, you need to calculate what your business is worth.

Your estate may also include other items that you don't have in your possession, such as:

Any future payments you expect to receive, such as an insurance settlement or the remaining 18 annual payments from that $35 million lottery jackpot that you won a couple of years ago

Future inheritances

A loan you made to your sister to help get her business started (that she plans to repay to you when her enterprise starts turning a profit.

For more help on this subject, check out *Estate Planning For Dummies*

CHAPTER TWELVE

INSURANCE

BASIC INSURANCE INFORMATION

LIFE INSURANCE

WHOLE LIFE

TERM LIFE

ANNUITIES

PREPAID BURIAL INSURANCE

LIFE INSURANCE (TEMPLATES)

PROPERTY INSURANCE (TEMPLATES)

Basics of Life Insurance

History of Life Insurance

With this insurance information, it will help you make a wise decision. There are different types of insurance plans. You may not know, but you should know, how much life insurance you will need to protect your family, financially, if you should die. How would the bills be paid or how would ongoing financial obligations be met, not to mention, how would funeral costs be paid. This is why life insurance is valuable to help protect your family.

Life Insurance

The purpose of life insurance helps to ensure that your family and loved ones are protected against financial hardship in the event of your death. The money your dependents receive is called death benefits and can be used to pay off debts, such as mortgage or credit cards bills; provide extra income to help pay ongoing household bills; pay for your children's education and pay funeral costs and other final expenses.

It is up to you to decide the type and the amount of life insurance that is best suited to your specific needs. If you want to cover funeral costs and other final expenses, you may need a plan with a high face value amount.

For estate planning, life insurance is a useful and flexible asset. Life insurance has been used to replace loss of income.

There are two common types of life insurance. There is Term Life Insurance and Whole Life Insurance.

Term Life Insurance

Term Insurance covers you for a limited term or a certain life stage, like when you children finish college or when you retire. The premium can increase with age, or the premium could stay the same, but the benefits may decrease. If no claim is made against the policy during the term, neither you or your beneficiary will receive any benefits after the policy is no longer in effect.

Renewable Term Life Insurance

There are various types of Term Life Insurance. There is a Renewable Term which automatically renews your coverage at the end of a certain period of time.

Decreasing Term Life Insurance

Another type of term insurance is "Decreasing Term Life," which provides a sound way to add to existing coverage if your need for coverage will decrease over time. As a means of keeping premiums affordable, the face amount gradually decreases over the years.

Term Life Insurance

Term life is "pure" protection with no added features that increase the cost. The premium is lower than whole life insurance and is for younger families and large financial obligations.

Whole Life Insurance

Whole Life Insurance, also called permanent insurance or cash value insurance. Whole Life insurance provides coverage similar to term insurance, with two key differences.

First of all, it is permanent and does not expire at the end of a specified term, if you pay the premium. It stays in effect your "whole" life. The insurer will return the face value of the policy to you once you have reached a predetermined age. Usually the premium is based on your age when the policy takes effect and stays the same for life.

Whole Life & Term Life Insurance

The second basic way the whole life differs from term life is its cash value feature. Part of your premium goes toward insuring your life while the rest of it is invested. The invested portion earns interest, which is how your policy "builds" cash value. Here are some of the advantages of the cash value features:

If you cancel your policy, you can receive the cash value amount as a lump sum payment. It is unwise to surrender your policy in the first few years, because it will have accumulated little or no cash value.

If you stop paying your premium, the accumulated cash value can pay them for you for a specified time, thereby keeping your coverage in force. Or your cash value may be used to provide a smaller amount of coverage for the rest of your life.

Using the cash value in your life insurance as collateral, you can borrow money from the insurance company. The loan is not subject to credit checks or other restrictions, as it would be with most financial institutions.

Whole Life Insurance Cash Value

The cash value of a whole life insurance policy is not the same as its face value benefit amount. There is an important distinction: The cash value is the amount available if you cancel a policy before its maturity, while the face amount is the money that will be paid at death or when the policy matures.

The money paid out by a whole life policy is not subject to federal income tax, according to current IRS rules, or the laws of probate. For this reason, many people find whole life insurance to be an important tool for tax and estate planning purposes.

Annuities

Annuities is not a life insurance. It is essentially a contract which guarantees an income will be paid for a period of time — even for life. When you purchase an annuity, you decide how much to contribute and how often. You may choose to pay a single premium or make periodic payments. Once you've begun paying premiums, the money you invest grows tax-deferred.

There are two types of annuities: fixed and variable.

a. With a fixed annuity, the insurance company is responsible for where your money will be invested.

b. With a variable annuity, you assume responsibility for investment decisions.

Three Part Annuity Contract

A typical annuity contract includes three parties:

a. The annuitant — the person on whose life the terms of the annuity are measured and to whom the income is paid.

b. The annuity owner — the person who has the rights to the contract, such as the right to name a beneficiary, and the right to assign the contract. The annuitant and the annuity owner can be the same person, but do not have to be. For insurance, a wife can own a contract with her husband as an annuitant.

c. The beneficiary — the person who will receive payment upon the death of the annuitant.

Annuitant Payments

The annuitant may choose to have income payments made in one of two ways — immediate or deferred.

a. The immediate annuity requires a "single premium" up front and begins paying right away — usually a month after the premium is deposited.

b. The deferred annuity accumulates principal and interest for payment at a designated future date. With this type of annuity, you may choose a "periodic payment" option, in which you make regular contributions.

Without careful planning, many people of retirement age face the possibility of running out of money during the remainder of their lifetime. That is why annuities, with an option of income for life, have become so popular.

To determine your specific life insurance coverage, it should equal five to seven times your annual gross income. This will help you maintain your family's lifestyle.

Prepaid Funeral Plan

A prepaid funeral plan consists of a contract and a funding mechanism to pay for the funeral or burial plan. Under state laws, the funeral home or cemetery places a percentage of the payment in a state regulated trust or purchases a life insurance policy with the death benefits assigned to the funeral home or cemetery. Most, but not all prepaid contracts guarantee that the price of the funeral or burial will cost no more at delivery than what was paid at the point of purchase.

Pre-Payment

To help ease their survivor's burden of making funeral-elated decisions and paying for their choices, "an increase number of people are planning their own funerals, designating their funeral preferences, and sometimes even paying for them in advance. The question, "Is prepaid funeral plan right for you and your family?"

Funeral Pre-Funding

There are concerns and The Federal Trade Commission's booklet, *Shopping for Funeral Services*, offers suggestions on the questions to ask if you decide to sign-up for a pre-paid funeral plan.

- What happens to the money you've prepaid?
- What happens to the interest income on money that is prepaid and put into a trust account?
- Are you protected if the firm you dealt with goes out of business?
- Can you cancel the contract and get a full refund if you change your mind?
- What happens if you move to a different area or die while away from home?

Remember, every state has different requirements for handling funds paid for prearranged funeral services. Also, some prepaid funeral plans can be transferred, but it can cost you, or your surviving relatives, more money to do so.

Online Sources:

"Pre-Paid Funeral Plans: Buyer Beware," ElderLaw Answers, updated May 2014, Accessed September, 2016

Better Business Bureau, "Pre-Paid Funeral and Burial Plans," January 23, 2014

PROPERTY INSURANCE POLICY LIST
(To be used as a "How To" Template)

PROPERTY INSURANCE

Company Name ____

Address ________________________City__________________State_____Zip_______

Address of Property Covered____

Agent ____

Office Phone__________________________________Cell_____________________

Primary Beneficiary____

PROPERTY LIST

Address of Property 1____

Company Name ____

Address ________________________City__________________State_____Zip_______

Agent ____

Office Phone__________________________________Cell_____________________

Primary Beneficiary____

Address of Property 2_______________________________________

Company Name ____

Address __________________________City_________________State_____Zip_______

Agent ____

Office Phone___________________________Cell_____________________

Primary Beneficiary______________________________________

Address of Property 3_______________________________________

Company Name ____

Address __________________________City_________________State_____Zip_______

Agent ____

Office Phone___________________________Cell_____________________

Primary Beneficiary______________________________________

CHAPTER THIRTEEN

ONLINE PROFILE

(TEMPLATES)

INTERNET

COMPUTERS

CELL PHONES

ONLINE PROFILES SHEET

BANKING ONLINE

Social Media Account Information, Computer Logins, Email Account Information

Log-in and password information for computers, email accounts, social media accounts, online banking and investment accounts, credit cards and autopay bill payments should be recorded and placed in a secure location. Family members should be made aware of this so they can take care of things should you become incapacitated.

Desktop Computer 1

UserID______________________________________

Password____________________________________

Desktop Computer 2

UserID______________________________________

Password____________________________________

Laptop Computer 1

UserID______________________________________

Password____________________________________

Tablet 1

UserID______________________________________

Password____________________________________

Tablet 2

UserID______________________________________

Password____________________________________

Cellphone User ID____________________________

Password____________________________________

Apple ID User Name___________________________

Password____________________________________

EMAIL ACCOUNTS

Account Location______________________________

UserID______________________________________

Password____________________________________

Answer to Recovery Question__________________

Account Location______________________________

UserID______________________________________

Password____________________________________

Answer to Recovery Question__________________

Account Location______________________________

UserID______________________________________

Password____________________________________

Answer to Recovery Question__________________

Account Location______________________________

UserID______________________________________

Password____________________________________

Answer to Recovery Question__________________

Account Location______________________________

UserID______________________________________

Password____________________________________

Answer to Recovery Question__________________

Account Location______________________________

UserID______________________________________

Password____________________________________

Answer to Recovery Question__________________

SOCIAL MEDIA ACCOUNTS

Social Media Account__________________________

Account Name__________________________

UserID__________________________

Password__________________________

Answer to Recovery Question__________________________

Cell Number __________________________

Social Media Account__________________________

Account Name__________________________

UserID__________________________

Password__________________________

Answer to Recovery Question__________________________

Cell Number __________________________

Social Media Account__________________________

Account Name__________________________

UserID__________________________

Password__________________________

Answer to Recovery Question__________________________

Cell Number __________________________

Social Media Account__________________________

Account Name__________________________

UserID__________________________

Password__________________________

Answer to Recovery Question__________________________

Cell Number __________________________

Social Media Account__________________________

Account Name__________________________

UserID__________________________

Password__________________________

Answer to Recovery Question__________________________

Cell Number __________________________

Social Media Account__________________________

Account Name__________________________

UserID__________________________

Password__________________________

Answer to Recovery Question__________________________

Cell Number __________________________

ONLINE BANKING AND INVESTMENT ACCOUNTS

Financial Institution________________________

Account Name________________________

UserID________________________

Password________________________

Answer to Recovery Question________________

Financial Institution________________________

Account Name________________________

UserID________________________

Password________________________

Answer to Recovery Question________________

Financial Institution________________________

Account Name________________________

UserID________________________

Password________________________

Answer to Recovery Question________________

Financial Institution________________________

Account Name________________________

UserID________________________

Password________________________

Answer to Recovery Question________________

Financial Institution________________________

Account Name________________________

UserID________________________

Password________________________

Answer to Recovery Question________________

Financial Institution________________________

Account Name________________________

UserID________________________

Password________________________

Answer to Recovery Question________________

CREDIT CARDS AND ONLINE SHOPPING ACCOUNTS

Web Address_______________________________

Account Name_______________________________

UserID_______________________________

Password_______________________________

Answer to Recovery Question_______________________

Web Address_______________________________

Account Name_______________________________

UserID_______________________________

Password_______________________________

Answer to Recovery Question_______________________

Web Address_______________________________

Account Name_______________________________

UserID_______________________________

Password_______________________________

Answer to Recovery Question_______________________

Web Address_______________________________

Account Name_______________________________

UserID_______________________________

Password_______________________________

Answer to Recovery Question_______________________

Web Address_______________________________

Account Name_______________________________

UserID_______________________________

Password_______________________________

Answer to Recovery Question_______________________

Web Address_______________________________

Account Name_______________________________

UserID_______________________________

Password_______________________________

Answer to Recovery Question_______________________

AUTOPAY BILL PAYMENT

Web Address_______________________________

Account Name_______________________________

UserID_______________________________

Password_______________________________

Answer to Recovery Question_______________

Web Address_______________________________

Account Name_______________________________

UserID_______________________________

Password_______________________________

Answer to Recovery Question_______________

Web Address_______________________________

Account Name_______________________________

UserID_______________________________

Password_______________________________

Answer to Recovery Question_______________

Web Address_______________________________

Account Name_______________________________

UserID_______________________________

Password_______________________________

Answer to Recovery Question_______________

Web Address_______________________________

Account Name_______________________________

UserID_______________________________

Password_______________________________

Answer to Recovery Question_______________

Web Address_______________________________

Account Name_______________________________

UserID_______________________________

Password_______________________________

Answer to Recovery Question_______________

Bibliography
(Resources)

Better Business Bureau, "Pre-paid Funeral and Burial Plans," January 23, 2014

Collins, Gary R., Ph.D., Christian Counseling: A Comprehensive Guide, Third Edition, 2007

Davis Funeral Homes & Memorial Park, 6200 South Eastern Avenue, Las Vegas, NV 89119, www.davisfuneralservices.com

Dove Releases Graveside, Love Doves 702-809-8580

Elder Law Answers, "Pre-Paid Funeral Plans: Buyer Beware," updated May 2014, Accessed September, 2016 (Online Source)

Evans, Jimmy with Martin Frank, *When Life Hurts*, Baker Books, Grand Rapids, Michigan

Health Care Partners, Five Wishes, A Medical Directive, Aging with Dignity, Supporting the Dignity and Advance Directives of our Patients throughout the Los Angles Area for Over 30 Years, 2007, 2009, www.dignitymemorial.com

Helping Yourself at Your Time of Loss, www.dignitymemorial.com, Helpful Dignity Memorial @ Network Resources and Services

Helping Yourself or a Coworker, Picking Up the Pieces, 2003, DignityMemorial.com@network, Inc.

Jones, Rebccca Rene, *Broken for Good, Faith Words*, Hackette Book Group, Inc. 2016.

Laws by State, https://eform.com

Lewis, C. S., *A Grief Observed*, Harper Collins Publications, 1980

Lewis, C. S., *Mere Christianity*, Harper Collins Publications, 1980

Lewis, C. S., *Surprise by Joy*, Harper Collins Publications, 1980

Living Will versus Medical Power of Attorney, https:// eform.com

Mitsch, Raymond R. and Brookside, Lynn, *Grieving the Loss of Someone You Love*, Regal, 1993

Omartian, Stormie, *Just Enough Light for the Step I'm On*, Harvest House Publishers, 1999/2008

Ten Things Everyone Should Know About Planning a Funeral or Cremation Service, Dignity Memorial, 2003, Dignity Memorial.com@Network, Inc.

Westburg, Granger E, *Good Grief*, 1997 Augsburg Fortress.

Who has the Legal Right to make Decisions about My Funeral? Affordable Cremation and Burial Service, www.addfordabllecremationlv.com, 2003, Dignity Memorial Network, Inc.